Seize the Day: 250 Anecdotes and Stories

David Bruce

Published by David Bruce, 2023.

While every precaution has been taken in the preparation of this book, the publisher assumes no responsibility for errors or omissions, or for damages resulting from the use of the information contained herein.

SEIZE THE DAY: 250 ANECDOTES AND STORIES

First edition. May 16, 2023.

Copyright © 2023 David Bruce.

ISBN: 979-8215573341

Written by David Bruce.

Table of Contents

Dedication

DEDICATED TO MY SISTER MARTHA

Martha wrote, "When I was working at Longaberger, I worked with a girl who had two children and was in the middle of a divorce. She was so worried about Christmas for her boys. I received a very nice Christmas bonus that year, and I went to my boss and started a donation fund for the girl. My boss told me later that she — my boss —delivered the money to the girl's mother and father and told them not to tell her who brought the money for her. Months later the girl told me that the boys had the best Christmas that year, and she told me someone had brought money to her mom and dad for her, and she went to town and bought the boys Christmas. She never did know who did that for her. She was so thankful. I believe that I was the only one who donated to her, which was just fine."

***

The doing of good deeds is important. As a free person, you can choose to live your life as a good person or as a bad person. To be a good person, do good deeds. To be a bad person, do bad deeds. If you do good deeds, you will become good. If you do bad deeds, you will become bad. To become the person you want to be, act as if you already are that kind of person. Each of us chooses what kind of person we will become. To become a good person, do the things a good person does. To become a bad person, do the things a bad person does. The opportunity to take action to become the kind of person you want to be is yours.

Bai Juyi went to Zen master Daolin of the Tang Dynasty and asked what one must do in order to live in accord with the Tao. Daolin answered, "One must avoid doing evil, and one must do as much good as possible." Bai Juyi was surprised at the simplicity of this answer and said, "Even a child knows that." "True," replied Daolin, "even a child of three knows this but even a man of 80 fails to live up to it."

A seeker after truth once asked a wise person how to seek God. The wise person replied, "The ways to God are as many as there are created beings. But the shortest and easiest is to serve others, not to bother others, and to make others happy."

Cover Photograph for *Seize the Day: 250 Anecdotes and Stories*
Front Cover Photo
https://pixabay.com/photos/father-and-son-baby-father-child-1153919/

***

This is a short, quick, and easy read.
Anecdotes are usually short humorous stories. Sometimes they are thought-provoking or informative, not amusing.

***

Educate Yourself
Read Like A Wolf Eats
Be Excellent to Each Other
Books Then, Books Now, Books Forever

***

Do you know a language other than English? If you do, I give you permission to translate this book, copyright your translation, publish or self-publish it, and keep all the royalties for yourself. (Do give me credit, of course, for the original book.)

Introduction: Seize the Day

• Cindy Jones is a nurse who works with cancer patients. In 1996, one such patient was about to die. One of Cindy's colleagues asked the woman, "What is important to you?" What was important to the woman was being married to her boyfriend, but the two had kept postponing the date. The staff at the hospital got busy. Because the woman and her boyfriend had little money, a fund the hospital kept to help patients was used to buy the wedding license. The hospital chaplain performed the ceremony. The hospital's medical media department photographer took the wedding photos. A white negligee served as a wedding dress for the woman. Sheets were hung to make the atmosphere less like that of a hospital. The woman was a very happy bride, and she died approximately four hours after becoming a wife. Ms. Jones wrote, "For years I have been wearing a button on my lab coat: 'Oncology [Cancer] Nurses Say Never Postpone a Pleasure.' For me, it sums up a philosophy I have developed after nearly two decades in my field. I am constantly reminded to try to live each day as if it were my last and to not have any regrets about things I wished I had taken the time to enjoy." This kind of advice is, of course, similar to the Latin *carpe diem*, which can be translated as "seize the day." So how can we seize the day? Some ways include living a life of wit and intelligence, practicing an art, doing good deeds, paying attention to your soul as well as your body, staying angry at the things that should anger us, and being aware of the fabulous realities that surround us despite the presence of evil in the world. Here are some bumper-sticker condensations of ancient and modern wisdom: Resist Psychic Death, Do It Yourself, Make Art, Don't Fear the Reaper, Maintain Maximum Cool, Do Good Now, and Reality is Fabulous.[1]

Chapter 1: From Activism to Critics

Activism

• Maury Maverick, Sr., was the mayor of San Antonio, but he was very outspoken for a politician. Once, politicians in San Antonio banned all outdoor eating establishments because they wanted to close down the chili queens operating in the streets. Soon after, Mayor Maverick attended a fancy outdoor garden picnic that was also attended by the politicians who had passed the ban, so he told his host, "You-all know it's against the law to have outdoor eating places. You bastards passed the law yourself. I'm giving this party 15 minutes to get these tents down and all this food indoors, or the police will be called!"[2]

• In 2011, the Planet Fitness chain of health clubs decided to go after the market of average Janes and Joes rather than people seeking a true weightlifting workout; therefore, Planet Fitness started using a series of television commercials depicting lunks (its word for bodybuilders and serious weightlifters) straining to do such tasks as tie their shoes. Outraged, the lunks fought back. Lunks joined together and shut down the Planet Fitness YouTube channel by continually flagging its commercials as offensive. Planet Fitness had to start a new channel under a different name.[3]

• Benjamin Lay was an 18th-century Quaker who preached against slavery. At a Quaker meeting, Mr. Lay waved a sword over his head as he shouted that slavery was just as pleasing to God as abusing the Bible would be. He then plunged the sword through a Bible. Previously, he had inserted in the Bible a packet of red dye resembling blood. The dye splattered people sitting nearby, and Mr. Lay told them that now other people could see the stain of their sin.[4]

• In 1899, miners went on strike in Arnot, Pennsylvania. Union organizer Mother Jones was there, and when the mining company brought in strikebreakers, Mother Jones organized an army of miners' wives to drive away the strikebreakers by attacking them with mops and brooms. The battle tactics worked, and in February of 1900, after a 10-month strike, the Erie Company met the union's demands and began to pay better wages.[5]

Actors

• Some actresses act even when they are not on stage or in front of a camera. Tallulah Bankhead once complained about a young actress who had a bit role in one of her plays. Ranting and raving, Ms. Bankhead strode up and down her dressing room complaining about the actress. The play's director, John C. Wilson, told her, "We've already fired that girl." Ms. Bankhead replied, "I know that, but for heaven's sake, let me have my scene."[6]

• Courtenay Thorpe was an actor who continued working in his profession with a false limb after his hand was blown off during an accident with a gun. A stage manager once told him that his hand seemed rather wooden when he gestured with it, and Mr. Thorpe replied, "That may be because it is chiefly made of wood."[7]

• Before Dick Van Dyke walked into an office to talk over what became *The Dick Van Dyke Show* with executive producer Sheldon Leonard and producer Carl Reiner, they were wondering how many people he would have in his entourage. They were pleasantly surprised when he came alone.[8]

• During a rehearsal of *The Darling of the Gods*, Herbert Beerbohm Tree asked an actor to stand back a little, then a little more, then a little more. The actor complained, "If I go back any more, I shall be right off the stage." Mr. Tree replied, "Exactly."[9]

Advertising

• For a show at the Aquarama at Flushing Meadow Park in New York, several casting ads in *Variety* appeared. The first ad said: "Aqua Circus in Flushing Meadow! Beauties wanted. Must be expert dancers and swimmers." One week later, the second ad said: "Wanted! Girls with good figures who can swim." Two weeks later, the third and final ad said: "Wanted! Girls with good figures who can swim a little." When the show was finally performed, the women who had been cast didn't swim — they paddled around on surfboards.[10]

• The ads for Bert and Harry Piel beer were so funny that customers rushed to buy the beer, but after tasting it, they hated the beer so much they never bought it again.[11]

Alcohol

• A man named Lamb once applied for a liquor license in Randolph County, Tennessee. Because the application for the liquor license had to be approved by the Board of County Commissioners, he hired an able lawyer to present his case. The lawyer argued long and well, and he emphasized that Mr. Lamb was of good character. After the lawyer had presented his case, an aged Quaker, who served on the Board of the Commissioners and who was a neighbor to Mr. Lamb, said, "I am glad indeed to know that my friend and neighbor has such an excellent character. So far as I am concerned, it shall remain good." The liquor license was not granted.[12]

• A Maharajah in India before World War II had an interesting way of fishing. He would have a drink and then walk down to the river, where one of his servants was standing with a fishing pole in whose hook had been caught a large fish. The Maharajah would reel in the large fish, then go to another servant, who was also holding a fishing pool in whose hook had been caught a large fish. When the Maharajah was finishing reeling in all the fish, he would go have another drink.[13]

• The New York *Herald Tribune* was a strictly Republican paper during Prohibition, but its editors and reporters liked to have a drink at Bleeck's, a nearby, illegal speakeasy. Ogden Reid, the publisher of the *Herald Tribune*, once warned the Republican administration in Washington, D.C., that if the police ever raided Bleeck's, the paper would immediately start supporting Democrats in political elections. Bleeck's was never raided.[14]

• Eddie Cantor once asked W.C. Fields why he never went swimming. Mr. Fields explained that while working in Atlantic City, he had to pretend to drown twelve times a day in front of a restaurant so that a huge crowd would gather, then seek refreshment. Mr. Fields told Mr. Cantor, "That's why I'm against water. I got enough in Atlantic City to last me a lifetime."[15]

• Archbishop Angelo Giuseppe Roncalli, later to be Pope John XXIII, was a master diplomat. At a diplomatic reception in Paris, an inebriated guest wanted Archbishop Roncalli to talk about a controversial area of religion. Archbishop Roncalli answered, "I never discuss religion at cocktail parties."[16]

• Zen master Bassui prohibited his students from drinking even a drop of alcohol, but later he got drunk in front of his students. When his students questioned him about his inconsistency, he said that he was teaching them not to get so hung up on rules![17]

• Peggy Cass once went on a trip to Germany, where she ordered a dry martini. The server returned with three martinis. As he set them before her, he said, "*Eins, zwei, drei* martinis."[18]

Authors

• After Amy Tan wrote her first book, the hugely successful *Joy Luck Club*, she worried that people would think that her second book was not as good as her first. In fact, Ms. Tan worried so much that at night as she lay sleeping she ground her jaws together, cracking two teeth! Before she had even written her second book, she learned that a woman in Columbus, Ohio, had stated in a discussion group meeting devoted to *The Joy Luck Club*, "Well, I just read Amy Tan's second book, and believe me, it's not *nearly* as good as the first!" Whatever book the Columbus, Ohio, woman had read, it was not Ms. Tan's second book. (By the way, when it was published, Ms. Tan's second book, *The Kitchen God's Wife*, received excellent reviews.)[19]

• Ian Fleming fell in love with Jamaica, and he built a house there, naming it "Goldeneye" after a wartime mission he had led during

World War II. Mr. Fleming and his men had crossed the English Channel to occupied France, where they had destroyed any enemy outlook posts they could find. By the way, Goldeneye was remarkably ugly when it was first built. Mr. Fleming's neighbor, Noel Coward, used to give these directions to people looking for it: "Straight on for miles, and it is the nearest ear, nose, and throat clinic on the right."[20]

• G.K. Chesterton was able to lose himself in a subject. A very overweight man, Mr. Chesterton was once sitting in a chair, discussing a subject, when the chair collapsed on him. He moved to another chair and continued the discussion at the exact word he had left off. The people present were convinced that he had barely noticed the collapsing chair and his move to a sturdier seat.[21]

Bathrooms

• Glyndebourne was a huge manor house in England. Because of worries about war in 1939, John Christie, the owner of Glyndebourne, had offered it as an evacuation center for London children. One day, buses arrived from London, and approximately 300 children and 72 adult caretakers got off the buses. Large as it was, Glyndebourne was unable to house that many people, and eventually the number staying there was lowered to 100. In the meantime, because of the lack of restroom facilities, Rudolf Bing, who helped manage the music festivals held at Glyndebourne, went into town and asked Woolworth's if it stocked chamber pots. Fortunately, it did, and he caused a sensation by buying six dozen.[22]

• When he was a Captain, British Admiral Sir Raymond Lygo was asked to be an after-dinner speaker for the Rotarians. During the dinner, the head Rotarian asked Sir Raymond's wife how long the speech would be and was shocked to hear that it would be 45 minutes. After the dinner, he announced to the diners, "Owing to the fact that the Captain's speech will last for 45 minutes, I can allow you only five minutes to relieve yourselves." Following the rush of the audience for the bathrooms and their return to the dining hall, the speech went well.[23]

• Saul Bellow and his literary agent, Harriet Wasserman, once had dinner at the home of Allan Bloom (also represented by Ms. Wasserman), who kept jumping up to get something from the kitchen. Each time he went past a palm tree that Mr. Bellow thought was very ugly, its fronds brushed his backside. Mr. Bellow watched this for a while, then he told Mr. Bloom, "Allan, now I know what that plant's good for."[24]

• Ferdinand IV, King of Naples, occasionally went to the theater. Whenever he did, his servants carried his portable toilet along so that he would not have to use public facilities. When the portable toilet was seen in the streets of Naples, soldiers saluted it, and officers drew their swords and stood at attention.[25]

Books

• G.K. Chesterton regarded *Napoleon of Notting Hill* as his first important book. To fortify himself for his meeting with his publishers, he took the little money he had left — for a while, he was an impoverished writer — and used it to get a shave, a huge luncheon, and a bottle of wine. Having fortified himself, he went to his publishers and asked for a £20 advance to write the book. The publishers said they would send it to him on Monday, but Mr. Chesterton said that if they wanted the book written, they would have to give him the money now as he was going to go away to write it. The publishers gave him the money. By the way, Mr. Chesterton's detective character "Father Brown" was based on a real-life priest, Father John O'Connor. Father O'Connor was once introduced as Father Brown to a couple of international thieves — who immediately disappeared, leaving no trace behind.[26]

• J.D. Salinger's title for *Catcher in the Rye* comes from Holden Caulfield's desire to stand in a field of rye by a cliff and protect the children as they play: "I have to catch everybody if they start to go over the cliff. I'd just be the catcher in the rye and all. I know it's crazy, but that's the only thing I'd really like to be." *Catcher in the Rye* became a main selection of the Book-of-the-Month Club, but its founder, Harry Scherman, asked Mr. Salinger to change the title of his novel to something less odd. Mr. Salinger declined, saying, "Holden Caulfield wouldn't like that."[27]

• While writing *The Wonderful Wizard of Oz*, L. Frank Baum needed to come up with a name for the magic land. He looked at a filing cabinet and saw three drawers listed A-G, H-N, and O-Z. O-Z? Problem solved. (Unfortunately, Mr. Baum's wife said that this story isn't true.)[28]

Christmas

• In 1986, Deborah Dunne was an OB nurse manager in a hospital on the East coast. During her rounds, she discovered a woman crying in the dark. Nurse Dunne talked with the woman and discovered that she had given birth to a premature baby boy who was in the Neonatal Intensive Care Unit, and she was terrified that her son would die. Nurse Dunne talked with the nurses in the NICU and made sure that it was an OK time for the woman to visit her baby, and then she took the woman in a wheelchair to the NICU. The woman talked to and caressed her son, and a NICU nurse talked to her and let her know that her son would be all right. For many years afterward, Nurse Dunne received a Christmas card from the woman, thanking her and giving her an update on the woman's healthy, growing son. Nurse Dunne said that the cards and notes are "incredibly heartwarming. After all, what I did was nothing that special. It was all in a day's work for a nurse."[29]

• Kids say (and write) the darndest things. For example, a person who goes by the name "Wuapinmon" while posting writes about his wife finding this written in their eight-year-old daughter's diary: "What I want for Christmas. I want a Dsi [a handheld game console], a half a million dollars, a new bike, Taylor Swift's new album, a tree house, new high tops and art supplies and that's it." And a person who posts under the name "The Fourth Nephite" writes about his (or her) five-year-old daughter helping an elderly woman working the cash register at a candy store to bag the family's purchases. The woman told the girl that she could get a job at the candy store when she turned 16, but the girl matter-of-factly replied, "Won't you be dead by then?"[30]

• According to Peter Ustinov, his reputation for being multi-lingual is exaggerated. In English, he explained, "That is a false legend built up by unscrupulous press agents. I can speak only French, German, Italian, Spanish, and Russian — and I can survive in Serbo-Croat; but then I have a great gift for survival." Ustinov directed the movie *Lady L*, starring Sophia Loren as an 82-year-old woman. In one scene, she accidentally pulled off a part of the mask that made her appear older. Mr. Ustinov said to her, "I told you not to open it till Christmas."[31]

• Frank Mullen lived in New York City one holiday season when the garbage workers were on strike and trash was piling up in the streets. He solved the problem of getting rid of his garbage by wrapping it up as if it were a Christmas present and leaving in the back of his unlocked car. Each time he did this, his garbage was stolen.[32]

Children

• Paul Candler Porter was the youngest child of a strict and loving preacher; he also had a strange sense of humor. One Sunday, his father stood in the pulpit and said, "Let us sing hymn number 135. Please stand on the last verse." When it was time to stand on the last verse, young Paul put his hymnbook — opened to hymn number 135 — down in the middle of the church aisle, then literally stood on the last verse.[33]

• As a result of having 20 children, Frank and Helen Beardsley appeared on *The Tonight Show with Johnny Carson*. Johnny asked, "How do you manage, having 20 children?" Mrs. Beardsley replied, "I'm doing what I enjoy most. I guess I was just made for it." Later,

Johnny told the audience, "I have only three children. I don't know how they do it." An audience member yelled, "Yes, you do!"[34]

• Abraham Lincoln was once seen with two crying children. When asked what was wrong, he answered, "The same thing that's wrong with the world. I've got three walnuts, and each child wants two."[35]

• A Bible class for first graders was reviewing the story of creation, so the teacher asked her young students how God had created Adam and Eve. One young pupil answered, "Naked."[36]

Church

• The Quakers maintained peace with the Native Americans in Pennsylvania, even when the Native Americans were warring with other white settlers. Some Native Americans in full war regalia once stopped at a Quaker Meeting House, looked inside, and saw the Quakers engaged in silent worship. The Native Americans entered the Meeting House, piled their weapons in a corner, and stayed for worship. Even during the wars between the Native Americans and other white settlers, the Quakers refused to lock the doors of their houses. During wartime, the Native Americans used to test the doors of settlers' homes. If the door of a house was unlocked, the Native Americans would leave that house and its inhabitants alone.[37]

• In Kentucky, by state law, a preacher can carry a concealed gun on church grounds. This has led Rev. Jeff Hanna, who is the pastor of the First United Methodist Church in Galion, Ohio, to wonder what kinds of things a pastor packing a gun might say. Perhaps: "Repent — or I'll shoot!" Or: "And now, which points of the sermon do you disagree with?"[38]

Clothing

• Tenor Enrico Caruso made fabulous amounts of money during his career, and he spent fabulous amounts of money. Once, he took his wife to a New York fur store and had her try on fur coats. She liked a small fur coat that cost much less than most of the others, but he asked her to try on more fur coats. Eventually, a dozen fur coats were piled around her. Mr. Caruso then told the saleslady, "Thank you. Very nice. Thank you very much. Very good. We take them all."[39]

• Actor Sheldon Leonard was surprised by the theatrical audiences in Palm Springs. While he was touring in *Margin for Error*, he noticed that on opening night the theater was packed with Palm Springs socialites, dressed to the hilt. However, after the intermission, the theater was half empty. This made Mr. Leonard worry, until the theater manager told him, "It's always that way. They come for the opening. The women see what all the other women are wearing and that's it. Off they go, back home."[40]

• In Paris, Angelo Giuseppe Roncalli, who was later to be Pope John XXIII, attended a reception at which the hostess wore a low-cut gown. Everyone watched Father Roncalli to see his reaction to the hostess' clothing, and he set everyone at ease by saying, "I can't imagine why all the guests keep looking at me, a poor old sinner, when my neighbor, our charming hostess, is so much younger and more attractive."[41]

• Traditionally, Quakers wear colors such as grey so as not to be guilty of vanity. Once, a Quaker known as Harvey the Scientist appeared at a Meeting and startled everyone by wearing clothing that was cut the traditional and proper way, but which was bright red. Very quickly, the matter was cleared up — Harvey the Scientist was colorblind.[42]

Crime

• God commands store owners to use fair weights. As part of his duties, Rabbi Eizel Charif used to go to the stores in his town and check all the weights twice a week to ensure that they were fair. One store owner complained about this, saying that he was a very busy man who did not have time to have his weights checked twice a week. The good Rabbi said that there was a way for the store owner not to be obligated to have his weights checked twice a week — he could instead hang this sign in front of his store: "This store is owned by a thief."[43]

• President John Adams enjoyed telling a story about a con man who sold flea powder. After some ladies had bought the flea powder, they asked the con man how to use it. He advised them to catch a flea, then pour the powder down its throat, and that would kill the flea. One of the ladies asked, "Since the flea is between your thumb and finger, why not squeeze it to death?" The con man gravely replied, "That would do as well."[44]

• During the Jewish Passover Seder, the door is opened to welcome the prophet Elijah. Once a Jewish prisoner complained to a rabbi that he was not allowed to observe his religious beliefs. This concerned the rabbi greatly, until he learned that the warden hadn't allowed the Jewish prisoner to open the door of the prison to welcome Elijah.[45]

Critics

• The emir of a town held a public reading of his poems. After reading the first poem, he asked Bahlul for his opinion. "Your poems stink," Bahlul replied. The emir immediately had Bahlul arrested and taken to prison. After Bahlul was released from prison, the emir held another public reading of his poems. Again, the emir asked Bahlul for his opinion. To the emir's surprise, Bahlul began walking away. "Where are you going?" the emir asked. Bahlul replied, "To the prison."[46]

• Fredrick the Second of Prussia once became angry because Moses Mendelssohn had criticized his poetry, so he sent Mendelssohn an insulting note. Later, Mr. Mendelssohn met the King and asked him to sign the note, which he did. Mr. Mendelssohn then read the note out loud: "Moses Mendelssohn is the first idiot in Prussia. Fredrick the Second."[47]

• Ambiguous statements can be insulting. Classical scholar Richard Porson was once told that poet Robert Southey had complained about one of his poems, "My 'Madoc' has brought me in a mere trifle; but that poem will be a valuable possession in my family." Dr. Porson commented, "'Madoc' will be read when Homer and Virgil are forgotten."[48]

• Dorothy Parker could be scathing in her condemnation of others, but there were some people she admired. When she first met detective novelist Dashiell Hammett, author of *The Maltese Falcon* and *The Thin Man*, she dropped to her knees, then kissed his hand. (He didn't like the public display of respect.)[49]

• John Parsons once was out riding with Lord Norbury, who was known as the Hanging Judge. They came across a gibbet, and Lord Norbury asked Mr. Parsons, "Where would you be now if that gallows had its due?" Mr. Parsons replied, "Riding alone, my lord."[50]

• Charles-Pierre Baudelaire and a friend were in an antique shop where a statue of a fat-bellied Buddha was displayed. On seeing the Buddha, the friend burst out laughing, but Mr. Baudelaire said, "Don't laugh. You may be in the presence of the true God."[51]

• Sometimes, critics are criticized. Elwyn A. Barron, the drama critic of the *Inter Ocean*, wrote a play. The Chicago *Tribune* reviewed it in this way: "At McVicker's Theatre last night was produced a play called *A Moral Crime*. It was."[52]

Chapter 2: From Death to Friends

Death

• As a young man, L. Frank Baum, who later wrote *The Wonderful Wizard of Oz*, almost fought a duel because of a typographical error. For his newspaper, the Aberdeen *Saturday Pioneer*, Mr. Baum wrote that a bride had a "roguish smile," but the typesetter accidentally changed it to "roughish smile." The angry bridegroom quarreled with Mr. Baum, and bystanders suggested that they fight a duel. They met outside the newspaper office and were supposed to walk around the block — each man in a different direction — until they met again behind the newspaper office, then they would start firing at each other. Mr. Baum, however, rounded the first corner, then started running for his life. He must have been a slow runner because a friend caught up with him and told him that the bridegroom was also running away. Hearing that, Mr. Baum returned to the scene of the duel and shouted, "Where is that coward? Lead me to him!"[53]

• Andrew Tobias and Charles Nolan were a happy gay couple for years until Mr. Nolan died. Soon after Mr. Nolan died, Mr. Tobias' mother, who was Jewish, also died. At the memorial service for Mr. Tobias' mother, Mr. Nolan's brother spoke. Mr. Tobias writes about "Charles' brother, a Catholic priest, who, when he got up from the audience to speak to the largely Jewish crowd, said he imagined my mom and dad and stepfather (also Jewish) and Charles (Catholic, but lapsed, and gay) — were now all likely in paradise having a fine and stylish old time together." Mr. Tobias noted to the Catholic priest (with a smile) that according to the Pope, perhaps none of them would gain admission to Heaven. Mr. Tobias writes, "To which he shot back — with a quiet conviction I get a little choked up recalling — 'It's not his call.'"[54]

• Here are three anecdotes about death and dying: 1) A physician told Lord Palmerston that he was dying. Lord Palmerston replied,

"Why, dying is the last thing that I shall do." 2) When Irish clown Johnny Patterson lay dying, his doctor told him, "I'll see you in the morning." Mr. Patterson smiled, then replied, "Sure, doc, but will I see you?" 3) James Joyce's father once read the obituary of a good friend, Mrs. Cassidy, to his wife. Mrs. Joyce said, "Don't tell me that Mrs. Cassidy is dead!" Her husband replied, "Well, I don't quite know about that, but someone has taken the liberty of burying her."[55]

• Occasionally, a newspaper makes a mistake — even the London *Times*. Lord Bessborough had died, but unfortunately the *Times* printed the obituary of Lord Desborough. That morning, the telephone rang at the *Times*, and a young employee named John Lawrence answered it. The voice on the telephone said, "Lord Desborough speaking. Look here, you've printed my obituary in the *Times* this morning!" Mr. Lawrence asked, "And where are you speaking from now, your Lordship?"[56]

• Zen Master Hakuin Ekaku saw a physician in the year 1768, who said he was fine, but Hakuin Ekaku said, "Some doctor. He can't see that in three days I'll be gone." Sure enough, three days later he died, leaving a final piece of calligraphy, in the center of which was a large character meaning "midst." The calligraphy read: "Meditation in the MIDST of action is a billion times superior to meditation in stillness."[57]

• A friend of meditation teacher Sharon Salzberg spent time contemplating skeletons — with interesting results. He says, "At first, it was absolutely disgusting, but over time, a special kind of clarity came — one of no pretense, no social niceties. I'd walk into the dining room and see myself as a skeleton and everyone else as a skeleton. It is just the way it is."[58]

• When the famous Yiddish humorist Sholom Aleichem died, Mendele Mocher Seforim, who was known as the Father of Yiddish literature, quoted from Psalms, "He that sitteth in Heaven laugheth," then added, "Now that Sholom Aleichem is in Heaven, God Himself is having fun."[59]

• A wealthy man died, leaving millions of dollars behind, and Mulla Nasrudin appeared at the funeral, crying bitterly. A friend told him, "You must be crying because the rich man was a relative." Nasrudin replied, "No, I am crying because the rich man was not a relative."[60]

• On his deathbed, George Buchanan, a Scottish churchman, was told that King James VI was angry at him because of his religious writings. He replied, "I am not much concerned about that, for I am shortly going to a place where there are few kings."[61]

• A man told Raba that the powerful mayor of a town had ordered him to kill someone, or he would be killed. Raba said, "Let the mayor kill you, but you must not kill. Do you think your blood is redder than another man's? Perhaps his blood is redder than yours."[62]

• While on his deathbed, Hui-yung suddenly asked for his clothes, and then he attempted to stand, all the time looking into space as if he were seeing something. His attendants asked what he was looking at, and he replied, "The Buddha is coming." Then he died.[63]

• When British actor Robert Morley, who was born in 1908, was growing up, the ultimate status symbol was when the authorities covered the streets with straw to reduce the noise while one was on one's deathbed.[64]

Education

• The first-ever class taught by Kari-Lynn Winters consisted of first-graders with behavioral problems; however, after the first day of class Kari-Lynn very seldom had any problem with any child. On the first day of class, Kari-Lynn passed out some candies that were to be used in a math lesson. She gave the children strict orders not to eat the candies yet, but a small girl did eat some candies and started choking. Kari-Lynn was so scared that she uttered some profanity in front of the children and then ran over, grabbed the child, and used the Heimlich maneuver (lifting the child off the ground as she did so) to get the candies out of the child's throat so the child could sit at her desk and breathe again. Kari-Lynn then telephoned the child's mother to come and pick up the child. That day she got a reputation as the school's strictest teacher. Students spread the word that you better not mess with Kari-Lynn because if you did, Kari-Lynn would do these things to you: 1) Cuss you out in front of the other children, 2) Grab you and lift you off the ground, 3) Break all your ribs, 4) Make you projectile vomit, 5) Sit you down at a desk and let you suffer from the pain of the broken ribs, and 6) Call your mother and tell on you so your mother would take you home and punish you again. After the first day of class, Kari-Lynn received many compliments on how well her students behaved.[65]

• Rabbi Ishmael was walking on a road when he met a sick man. Seeing a farmer working in a field nearby, he asked him to get a physician for the sick man. However, the farmer refused, saying that the man's life was in the hands of God. If God wanted the man to live, he would live; but if God wanted the man to die, he would die. Rabbi Ishmael pointed out that the growing of crops was in the hands of God. If God wanted the crops to grow, they would grow; but if God wanted the crops to die, they would die. Nevertheless, the farmer used a plow and planted seeds, showing that he was in a partnership with God to make crops live. So it is with a physician, who works in a partnership with God to make men live. After hearing this, the farmer summoned a physician.[66]

• Some people resist good ideas. In the late 1860s, the American Medical Association decided to advocate the raising of standards for the education of physicians by recognizing the schools that met stricter standards and not recognizing the schools that didn't. Harvard raised its standards, requiring oral and written exams in several areas of study, terms lasting nine months each, and three years of study. Students' reaction was decisive — during the years following the raising of standards, Harvard medical school enrollment dropped by 43 percent. Many students decided instead to attend medical schools with lower standards. (But by the 1920s, higher standards were in place everywhere in the United States.)[67]

• A rich man had a bad son. The rich man, thinking incorrectly that his son was a good man, gave him all his property. Immediately, the son began to treat the father poorly. Eventually, after years of neglect, the father was clad in rags. He begged his son for a cloak to keep him warm, and the son relented, telling his own small boy to get a certain cloak to give to the boy's grandfather. The small boy left to get the cloak, cut it in half, and brought half of the cloak back, explaining that he would give half of the cloak to his grandfather now and the other half of the cloak to his father later. The rich man's son realized how poorly he had been treating his father (and how poor an example he had been setting for his son), and he immediately began to treat his father with honor.[68]

• G.K. Chesterton was lecturing on Dante at California's Milbrook Junior College, when a woman who had lost her place in her volume of Dante, who had written about an imaginative journey through the afterlife, including Hell, called out, "Where the hell are we?" The class laughed, but Mr. Chesterton took the interruption with good humor, saying, "I rather like that phrase. Good Catholic expression. A Catholic doesn't live in Milbrook or in England, but *sub specie aeternitatis* [under the form of eternity], and the question always is, where in hell are we? Or where in heaven are we? Or where in purgatory are we? We live in that spaceless, timeless commonwealth and the question is very important."[69]

• After 28 medical schools rejected her application, Elizabeth Blackwell was very happy when she was finally accepted as a medical student at Geneva College. However, when she arrived in November 1847 to take classes, she discovered that she had been admitted to the medical school as a joke. No one had actually expected her to show up! Nevertheless, she persevered, although she was sometimes barred from laboratories and lectures by students — and sometimes by professors. In 1849, Ms. Blackwell became the first woman to graduate from medical school — at the top of her class, no less — and become a physician.[70]

• When Maya Angelou graduated from the 8th grade, a white education official came to her segregated school and talked about the improvements that would be made to local schools. He said that the white school would get new equipment for science labs and money for art programs, while the black school would get better sports facilities. This bothered young Maya because it seemed that white students could have the ambition of becoming another Galileo or Gauguin, while the black male students (at the time, few girls played organized sports) had to settle for trying to become sports stars.[71]

• The Emperor of Ryo wanted to learn about Zen Buddhism, so he asked Zen master Fu-daishi to explain the Diamond Sutra to him on a certain day. Fu-daishi arrived on the appointed day and stood behind the speaker's table. Without saying anything, he rapped on the table, then left. Another Zen master, Shiko, witnessed the demonstration, and he asked the Emperor of Ryo, "May I be so bold, sir, as to ask whether you understood?" The Emperor shook his head, No, and Shiko said, "What a pity! Fu-daishi has never been more eloquent."[72]

• Frederick Andrews was a 14-year-old head boy when he was asked to take the place of an absent teacher apprentice. Immediately, he began to abuse his power. He picked a fight with a student, then boxed the student's ears. Unfortunately, the student fell to the ground and lay still as if he were dead. Young Andrews began to worry about a coroner's inquest, but was relieved when the student suddenly jumped up and confessed that he had been acting. For the next 50 years of his teaching career, Mr. Andrews was careful not to abuse his power over students.[73]

• Rabbi Shalom Rokeach left his village at times to journey to visit the Seer of Lublin. Once, the Maggid of Kozienice asked him to stay in the village, promising that he would see the prophet Elijah if he stayed. Rabbi Shalom declined to stay. The Maggid of Kozienice again asked him to stay, promising that he would see the Patriarchs. Rabbi Shalom again declined. The Seer rejoiced to see Rabbi Shalom and said, "One who deprives oneself of the privilege of beholding Elijah and the Patriarchs in order to return to his teacher, is indeed a true Hassid."[74]

• Arthur Jerome Wright, the father of Marian Wright Edelman, believed passionately in education. When he died, the soles of his shoes had holes, but two of his children had graduated from college, another child was in college, and yet another child was in divinity school. His dying words to his daughter, Marian Wright Edelman, were, "Don't let anything get in the way of your education." In 1963, she received her law degree from Yale University, and in 1973, she founded the Children's Defense Fund, which lobbies politicians to pass legislation to help children.[75]

• A junior high student asked a teacher, "Would you answer a question about sex?" She asked in turn, "Don't you have a health teacher?" He replied, "Yes, but I'd rather ask you." Reluctantly, she said, "All right. What is it?" The boy replied, "I don't have a question right now." Later, the boy and several of his friends approached the teacher. The boy asked, "Didn't you say that you would answer any question that I had about sex?" The teacher said, "Yes," and the boy told his friends, "See! I told you she would," and then he and his friends walked away.[76]

• In 1903, Dr. Kaufmann Kohler became President of Cincinnati, Ohio's Hebrew Union College. A youthful guide named Samuel Caplan took a group of people around to see the sights of the college, and coming to Dr. Kohler's house, he announced, "This is where Dr. Kohler lives." He then picked up some gravel and threw it against an upstairs window. Instantly, the angry face of Dr. Kohler appeared. Mr. Caplan turned to his group and announced, "And that is Dr. Kohler."[77]

• R' Yitzchak Meir of Gur once asked a young chasid, "Do you know the Torah?" How to answer such a question was perplexing. On the one hand, if he said he knew a lot of Torah, he would appear to be boasting, and after all, R' Yitzchak Meir knew much more than he. On the other hand, he would be lying if he were to say that he knew nothing of the Torah. Therefore, he answered, "I know a little." R' Yitzchak Meir replied, "And who knows more than a little?"[78]

• Rabbi Baer of Radoshitz once asked his teacher, the Seer of Lublin, to show him "one general way to the service of God." The Seer replied, "It is impossible to tell men what way they should take. For one way to serve God is through learning, another through prayer, another through fasting, and another through eating. Everyone should carefully observe what way his heart draws him to, and then choose this way with all his strength."[79]

• Maya Angelou decided not to become involved with heavy narcotics in her life. A friend named Troubadour Martin was a user, and he let her see the lifestyle. She watched as he and his friends shot heroin into their veins, and then he told her to stay away from heavy narcotics. She did, and she credits her choice to his generosity in revealing this truly bad lifestyle to her.[80]

• Ikkyu wished to study Zen with master Kaso, so he appeared at the temple gate, where Kaso emptied a bucket of slop water on his head — a true Zen tradition. For three days, Ikkyu waited outside the temple gate, while Kaso decided whether to accept him as a disciple. After three days, Kaso welcomed Ikkyu as a disciple.[81]

• Back when IBM executive Carl Griffin was dating Christine Johnson, the principal of Abraham Lincoln High School in Denver, CO, they began to talk about having children. She told him, "Carl, I've got a couple of thousand kids." He says, "That's one of the reasons I fell in love with Christine." Later, they married.[82]

• While running for exercise, philosopher Richard Watson thinks. One topic he has thought about is what might be the defining characteristic of a philosopher. He reached the tentative conclusion that the defining characteristic of a philosopher is that the philosopher schedules time to think each day.[83]

• According to the Dalai Lama, we should be concerned with other people's happiness. If we are delighted with the happiness of other people and not just with our own happiness, then our chances of being delighted are increased to over six billion instead of just one.[84]

• A man improved his field by taking stones out of it; however, he tossed the stones onto a public road. Eventually, he sold his field, walked on the public road, and tripped over the stones he had thrown onto it.[85]

• Izu was a stern Zen master. He used to keep a sword near him whenever people wanted to ask him about Zen. If anyone tried to argue with him, he used his sword to chase them out of the room.[86]

• In 1907, Virginia Wolff tried teaching, but she didn't like it. She once wrote a lecture that began, "The poet Keats died when he was 25; and he wrote all his work before that."[87]

Fathers

• College seniors in bad economic times have a hard time getting jobs and sometimes move back home after graduating. As a senior, the daughter of Sanford Pinsker sent out many, many resumes and job-application letters and collected many, many rejection letters — so many, in fact, that she thumbtacked them on a wall that she called her "Wall of Shame." At one point, she wrote a letter to her parents asking them to allow her to move back home after she graduated. Her father wrote back, "Dear Ms. Pinsker: We have read your application with interest and agree that you have stellar credentials. Unfortunately, the position you want has already been filled. We will keep your letter on file and, should the situation change, we will be in touch. Respectfully yours, Your Father." She laughed and then thumbtacked this rejection letter in a place of honor on the wall. Some people who read the letter thought that her father must be a mean man, but she did get a job and she did not move back home. Mr. Pinsker writes, "I consider myself an 'enabler' in the best sense of the word, because I gave her a laugh and because I provided the prodding she may, or may not, have needed."[88]

• In May 2011, Stefanie Gordon was on a Delta airplane when the space shuttle *Endeavour* blasted into space. She had an iPhone, and she used it to take some amazing photographs of the *Endeavour* as it went by the airplane — amazing photographs that she uploaded to Twitter and that quickly went viral with over 650,000 views within a couple of days. Major media contacted Ms. Gordon to ask to reprint her photos, and Ms. Gordon quickly agreed, requesting only that they acknowledge her as the photographer. Most media obeyed, and some (such as the Associated Press) even paid her for the use of her photographs. Ms. Gordon did get one other benefit from the photographs: She says, "Dad is finally OK with me being on Twitter."[89]

• PopMatters' Senior Editor Karen Zarker asked Simon Van Booy, author of the novel *Everything Beautiful Began*, about "The latest book or movie that made you cry?" He replied, "'Captain Kitty's First Adventure' is a book about a cat that becomes a sea captain, despite being scared of water. That book made me cry, not only because it's first-rate storytelling and illustrating, but because my daughter wrote it and bound it with string as a Father's Day present."[90]

Food

• Trisha Yearwood displays a good sense of humor in her cookbooks. She writes that her recipe for Cowboy Lasagna "Serves 12 regular people or 1 hungry cowboy and his wife!" (She is married to fellow country singer Garth Brooks. He requested a "heartier, meatier lasagna, and Cowboy Lasagna, with its sage-flavored sausage and pepperoni, is the result.) She also writes, "Our daughter August isn't a chocolate fan (insert audible gasp here!)." And, of course, she named one of her cookbooks *Georgia Cooking in an Oklahoma Kitchen*. (She grew up in Georgia, and her husband grew up in Oklahoma.)[91]

• A young man wanted to study under the Sha'agas Aryeh; however, the Sha'agas Aryeh asked the young man a few questions and discovered that he was ignorant. Therefore, the Sha'agas Aryeh asked, "In what school did you eat?" The young man was surprised by the question and asked, "Don't you mean in what school did I learn?" "No," said the Sha'agas Aryeh. "I am certain that you ate, but I am not certain that you learned."[92]

• Sister Mary E. Penrose, OSB, of the St. Scholastica Monastery in Duluth, Minnesota, once was clearing away some plates following a meal at the monastery. As she put an empty platter on a cart, another sister apologized, saying, "There's no coffee cake left." Sister Mary replied, "Coffee cake? No, that was *stollen*" (a German delicacy). "Oh, really?" said the other nun. "That's too bad, because we ate it all."[93]

• A King invited his subjects to a banquet and told them to each bring a flask of wine to be poured into a large vat to be shared. One of his subjects decided to cheat and bring water, not wine, in his flask, reasoning that one flask of water in all that wine would be unnoticed. When all the flasks had been emptied into the vat, the King tasted the liquid — it was water. All of his subjects had decided to cheat.[94]

• Philosophy historian Frederick Copleston had an Aunt Edith who was very absent-minded. Once she and her husband, Reginald, were dining at the home of some friends when she tasted the soup, then told her husband, "We really must change the cook, my dear; this soup is quite tasteless."[95]

• Philosopher David Hume was thin as a young man. However, when he was in his twenties, he endured an emotional crisis because of his philosophical skepticism, and he ate so much that he gained 60 pounds in six weeks. For the rest of his life, he was a fat, but happy, man.[96]

• Donald Houston was asked his opinion about the survivors of an airplane crash who had resorted to cannibalism to survive. He replied, "I think they started off on the wrong foot."[97]

• Frank Harris once boasted of all the famous houses he had dined at in London. Oscar Wilde replied, "Yes, my dear Frank, we believe you. You have dined in every house in London — once."[98]

Friends

• Harold Ross, editor of *The New Yorker*, once wanted to go the theater with Marc Connelly, the playwright. Therefore, Mr. Ross broke a previous dinner engagement he had made with critic Alexander Woollcott — but without explaining why. Unfortunately, Mr. Ross and Mr. Connelly dined at the Algonquin Hotel — where they were seen by Mr. Woollcott, who was insulted. Later that night, Mr. Woollcott received this telegram: "Dear Aleck, I find myself in a bit of a jam. If anyone asks you where I was tonight would you mind saying I was with you? [signed] Ross."[99]

• Diana Rigg and Patrick Macnee starred together for two years in *The Avengers*, but only Mr. Macnee went on to star in *The New Avengers* a few years later. An American friend of Ms. Rigg's asked what he was doing professionally, and Mr. Macnee explained that he would soon be starring in *The New Avengers*. The American friend asked, "With Diana, of course?" Mr. Macnee was forced to say, no. The American friend, who was not known for her tact, said, "Then it's not worth doing, is it?" This made Ms. Rigg smile.[100]

• As a small Quaker boy, William H. Sessions enjoyed going to Harrogate Monthly Meeting because a friend of his mother's, Jane Pickard, used to play with him after the meeting. To show his appreciation, he wrote her a letter. He gave the letter to his father to mail, and his father thought about correcting the spelling errors in it, but decided, "No! It will give more enjoyment as it is." The beginning of the letter said, "Dear Fiend."[101]

Chapter 3: From Gays and Lesbians to Money

Gays and Lesbians

• Terry Ryan is one-half of the lesbian cartooning team T.O. Sylvester. (The other half is Sylvia Mollick.) Among Ms. Ryan's leisure activities is lying on the couch while "looking remarkably lifelike." By the way, lesbian cartoonist Angela Bocage, creator of *(Nice Girls Don't Talk About) Sex, Religion, and Politics*, jokes that one of her accomplishments was remembering to wear clothes when she attended her classes at law school. Also by the way, lesbian cartoonist Kris Kovick drew even as a child at age five or six. Her parents used to call the figures in Kris' drawings "little men," and little Kris was not then assertive enough to correct them by saying, "That's lesbians."[102]

• In New York, several people were marching under the Harvard banner. A Harvard man from the class of 1952 saw the banner and asked what it was for. Being informed that it was for a Pride March, he and his wife started marching, too. Later, they discovered that it was a *Gay* Pride March and quickly dropped out. By the way, at a party in Beverly Hills, someone said, "This is really fag city." Financial writer Andrew Tobias overheard him and said that the situation was worse than the person thought — he (Andrew) was gay, too.[103]

• Divine was a gay actor who dressed in women's clothes. A true original, Divine once made a date with a girl, then dressed in drag and went to her house to pick her up for their date. Divine said later that her parents were "real nice."[104]

Gifts

• The husband of Jodi R. Scott wanted to get his license to be a principal so he went back to school. This meant that he had to quit his job as a teacher and move to an apartment close to the school he would be attending. It also meant that he would be two hours away from his wife, Jodi, and their two daughters: Delcina (age 6) and Heather (age 3). As you would expect, this put stress on Jodi, as both she and their daughters missed him. Jodi's mother-in-law (Jo) and sister-in-law (Annie) knew that Jodi would be under stress so they sent her a we-care package. Jodi writes that the package was "full of little things to help me cope. Each item had a cute note attached. Example: One book with the note 'to escape reality,' and another worn book with 'this one has seen its share of stress,' body scrub 'to scrub away the blues,' and many more. Enclosed was a little card saying they loved me and were thinking of me. I cried when I opened it. It was a gift from the heart, and it made all the difference in the world to know that they understood and were supportive."[105]

• One of Xu Wenchang's friends decided to test his intelligence. The friend tied several presents at the top of a long pole, then he told Xu Wenchang, "If you can reach the presents without standing on a ladder or bending the pole or making the pole horizontal, the presents are yours." Xu Wenchang put the bottom of the pole in a well, and he easily reached the presents.[106]

Good Deeds

• In early 2010, a woman named "Sandy" (a pseudonym) had a good life in Chicago. She was a banker, and she had a 10-year-old son and a home. But in late 2010, she did not have a good life. She had lost her job, she had lost her home, and the Department of Children and Family Services had threatened to take away her son because Sandy and he were sleeping in a truck. Fortunately, a kind social worker moved her and her son to a hotel. The kind social worker even used her own money to pay for a few nights' stay in the hotel. Since then, someone else has been paying the hotel bill so that Sandy and her son don't have to live in her truck. That someone else is Curtis Jackson, who has been homeless since 2004. Each day, he begs for money and then goes to Sandy's hotel and pays her bill. Why? Simply because she was kind to him when she had a good job and a home. Mr. Jackson said, "All I can do is get out there and put a sign in my hand, or put a cup in my hand and ask people to help me out, and everything I get, except maybe bus fare and something to eat, I give it to her." He carries a bucket filled with the money people give him, and each night he empties the bucket on the counter of the hotel. From December 2010 to May 2011, he raised $9,000 to support Sandy and her son. Sandy said, "I've donated to charities, I've helped other homeless families — never realizing that one day we'd be in this situation. So thank God that we did have an angel waiting for us." Mr. Jackson said, "I have God. I'm one of the richest mans on this earth, 'cause I have God. Money is not my master. That's what's wrong with this world: money is its master." He added, "I'm out here for a purpose: to help someone, and that's all I'm trying to do is help someone that needs help right at this moment. And once she doesn't need help anymore, I'll move on to something else."[107]

• On April 16, 2011, a Middle Eastern businessman left a small fortune in the back of a taxicab that fortunately was driven by an honest man. Nigel Lipscombe, age 54, dropped off the businessman in Cambridge, Cambridgeshire, England, and then discovered that the passenger had left something behind. Mr. Lipscombe said, "Another passenger got in and asked if it was my bag on the back seat. I told him it was the last passenger's, and I took it. When I looked in, I could see a laptop and what felt like some documents but I didn't unzip the compartment to look. I went to the police station and the man was just coming out. [After he saw me, h]e was jumping about with delight." The rucksack contained £31,000 — a year and a half's wages to Mr. Lipscombe — but he said, "I wouldn't have kept it. I've always been an honest man. I wouldn't do it if it was a million pounds." His partner, Doreen Kavanagh, 42, said, "He did the right thing. I could have taken my kids to Disneyland. The girls are 21 and 22 now, but we always dreamed of going. We just never had the money." The Arab businessman gave Mr. Lipscombe a $200 tip, but added $300 after Mr. Lipscombe joked, "Is that all I get?" A spokesman for Cambridgeshire

Constabulary stated, "A man came into Parkside police station at 7.45pm on Saturday, April 16, with three friends and reported he had left a bag with $50,000 in it, €1,000 [Euros], a laptop, and his passport. We took a note and he left the station when the taxi driver pulled up outside with the bag. They all came into the station. We gave the man strong words of advice about carrying such a large amount of cash."[108]

• British couple Kevin Barclay and Sharon Wood used to smoke dozens of cigarettes a day, but they quit smoking after a veterinarian told them that their smoking was bad for the health of their pet parrot. The veterinarian, Glen Cousquer of the South Beech Veterinary Surgery in Essex, southeastern England, said, "One of the key things that we need to get right with parrots generally is air quality. This particular bird presented with very severe respiratory problems. The owners were instructed to do everything they could to improve the bird's environment. I think I must have shaken the owners up quite badly, because the next time I saw them they actually had booked themselves into one of these anti-smoking clinics and were determined to stop. They've gone five weeks." The couple's quitting smoking has helped their parrot, whose name is J.J. According to the veterinarian, the parrot "is doing really well. It is certainly going to improve his life expectancy." (Ditto for the parrot's owners.)[109]

• In New York City, a man named Sergio Robin, his sister (Fran), his mother, and his mother's friend (Toni) were heading out to dine at a restaurant together. Toni found a pocketbook on the sidewalk on E. 48th St between Lexington Ave. and 3rd Ave. Inside the pocketbook were money, a cell phone, a wallet, and so on. Toni began to call people whose telephone numbers were in the cell phone in hopes of finding the owner of the pocketbook. Eventually, she contacted someone who then contacted the owner of the pocketbook. The group went to a restaurant and dined, and the husband of the owner of the pocketbook came to the restaurant to pick up the pocketbook. Sergio wrote, "We all commended Toni on her full and complete honesty and the good deed she had performed. By the way, the husband was grateful enough also to invite us to a bottle of wine at our table. A good night was had by all, and Toni should be especially commended for her honesty and diligence in getting that pocketbook into its owner's hands."[110]

• In November 2005 in Los Angeles, Haider Sediqi found in his Checker taxi a pouch that a passenger had left behind. Mr. Sediqi went about his business as usual, and then he asked a friend whom he had met for lunch to look in the pouch for anything that would identify its owner. The friend looked and then said, "Oh, God. Look at those things." Inside the pouch were approximately 100 cut diamonds — worth $350,000. Also inside the pouch was a cell phone bill. Mr. Sediqi, an immigrant from Afghanistan, called the number on the cell phone bill and asked, "Um, did you leave anything?" The man who had left the diamonds behind was Eric Austein. Mr. Sediqi turned the diamonds over to the police, who confirmed the identity of Mr. Austein, who then took possession of the diamonds. Mr. Austein hugged Mr. Sediqi and promised him a reward. Mr. Sediqi said that he was not tempted to keep the diamonds, adding, "God is up there. He always watches."[111]

• The wife of a man named Tony lost her wallet at Wal-Mart in Woodstock, GA. Tony telephoned Wal-Mart to see if anyone had turned in the wallet, but nobody had at that time. However, two days later he and his wife went back to Wal-Mart and discovered that her wallet had been found and turned in to the lost-and-found, most likely by an employee who gathers shopping carts in the parking lot. Tony wrote, "The wallet had nothing missing, including over $50 cash. Apparently, the attendants at this particular store find three or four wallets a day and take pride turning them in with all contents intact. What customer service and character!"[112]

• Two men, a father and his son, had a dispute, so they came to R' Yehudah of Vilna, aka Yesod, for arbitration. The two men were poor, and they had only one coat, so they were arguing about who should wear it. The father argued that he was old and he needed the coat, and the son argued that he had to work outside and he needed the coat. Yesod listened to the two men, then told them to return the next day for his decision. After the two men had left, he ordered that a second coat be made. The next day, he told the two men, "You are both right. Here is another coat. Now you can both enjoy the warmth."[113]

• The father of a woman who posts at Helpothers.org under the name "SadieMadison" tells about her father, who saw a woman who looked confused at a Social Security office. He approached her and asked her if she needed help. She was deaf but could read lips, and he took her by her arm, led her to a Social Security official, explained that she was deaf and needed assistance, and then returned to his seat. The deaf woman thanked him in sign language. SadieMadison writes, "Having witnessed the small act of kindness, the rest of the waiting room erupted in applause."[114]

• In 1960, a burglar made the mistake of trying to burgle actor John Wayne's home. Mr. Wayne was home, and he grabbed a shotgun and chased the burglar into the backyard where he made the burglar stop by yelling, "I got you covered!" Mr. Wayne's wife telephoned the police, who quickly arrived. The burglar did have a request that he asked Mr. Wayne to fulfill: "I came here in a cab. The taxi driver is still outside. The meter's running. He didn't know I came to rob you. Could you take care of him, Mr. Wayne?" Mr. Wayne paid the taxi driver.[115]

• Good deeds need not cost much money. A person who goes by the online name of Ritac often walks (for health purposes) in a mall that has a merry-go-round whose rides cost $1.25. She often gives the operator of the merry-go-round $5 and tells the operator to give a ride to any child who looks as if he or she really wants to ride the merry-go-round. And whenever Ritac is at an amusement park she will buy extra tickets for rides and hand them out to children — and sometimes to elderly people.[116]

• Before World War I, singers were often paid for performing at benefit concerts. Enrico Caruso was once supposed to sing with fellow opera stars Marcella Sembrich and Antonio Scotti in a benefit concert, but he found out that the organizer was afraid that the expense of hiring three opera stars would make the concert too expensive to turn a profit for charity, Mr. Caruso said, "Don't worry any more. I will sing free."[117]

Halloween

• A person who goes by the moniker Anwahs writes about a bad deed and a good deed that occurred on Halloween in the year 2007. She accompanied her son as he went trick-or-tricking. Also trick-or-tricking were two girls: one a little older and one a little younger. Two teenage thugs stole the girls' bags of candy and ran away. (The bags were almost filled with candy.) The older girl ran after the boys, and the younger girl cried. Anwahs' son gave the younger girl *all* of his candy. Lots of people witnessed the theft, and lots of people chipped in with candy, and in the end everyone had lots of candy. Anwahs lives in a small town where everyone knows everyone, so the two teenage thugs were identified and sentenced to community service. And Anwahs is proud of her son.[118]

Heroes

• In August 1953, Pete Schoening was part of a group of seven mountain climbers who wanted to be the first to reach the top of K2, the world's second-highest peak, which is located in the Himalayas. A blizzard struck. One of the climbers, Art Gilkey, developed a dangerous blood clot in his lungs. The other climbers tried to carry him down the mountain using a technique called the "belay," which involves suspending the person from a rope. Going down the mountain, George Bell slipped. He pulled most of the others down with him, but they were connected with a rope to Mr. Schoening, who stopped their slide by holding fast to an ice pick. The men were dangling thousands of feet in the air. Later, Mr. Gilkey died (he may have deliberately cut the ropes securing him, in order to save the others), but the others all survived. Climber Dee Molenaar said, "I'm sure we would have all gone down [if not for Mr. Schoening]. He was a prince of a human being." In 1978, Mr. Schoening told a *Seattle Times* reporter, "When you get into something like mountain climbing, I'm sure you do your thing automatically. It's a mechanical function you've been trained to perform. You do it when necessary without giving it a thought of how or why."[119]

• In September 2005, Allen Wylde-Browne rescued a 12-year-old boy who had fallen into the sea at Port Macquarie, located just north of Sydney, Australia. The boy and his father had been walking in a rocky area at Nobbys Beach when the boy lost his balance and fell into the water, injuring himself. Allen said, "When I saw the kid, he was holding onto some rocks and only his head was above the water. I didn't really think about it, but I knew if I climbed down to where he was, I could probably pull him out. I climbed over to where he was and told him that it was going to be OK. He kept saying he was going to die and that he couldn't really breathe. I told him he wasn't going to die and that if he could just push himself up a little bit I could get him." The boy did push himself up, and Allen grabbed him, helping to keep his head out of the water. Allen said, "After that more people had been called and another guy came along and was able to pull him right out of the water." Allen added, "I stayed with the kid till the ambulance officers arrived and took over. It felt really good to be able to help, but I don't feel like a hero — it was just a quick decision."[120]

• In August 2005 in Brooklyn, New York, a 6-year-old girl named Karizma Cox fell from a day care's third-floor rooftop playground. With her grandmother, she had checked out of Flatbush's Initial Steps Child Development Center, but she returned alone to the playground where she had left some cookies. The door locked behind her, and she tried to climb down but fell. Fortunately, Mohammed Azaze Balde had climbed onto a fire escape two stories high and caught her, although she did hit the railing. Mr. Balde, age 25, an immigrant from Guinea in West Africa, had been driving to pick up Chinese food when he saw the little girl in a dangerous situation. He said, "I saw her and I said to myself, 'I have to save her life.' I decided that I couldn't wait. I knew if I wasted any time, it was going to be dangerous." He ran up the fire escape steps and then caught her as she fell. Vanessa Cox, age 30, Karizma's aunt, said, "I'm just so glad he reacted and wasn't one of the people that just sat there and looked." Karizma was taken to Kings County Hospital, but was soon laughing and talking.[121]

• As a conductor of the Underground Railroad, escaped slave Harriet Tubman courageously rescued over 300 people from slavery. In doing so, she had to worry about people becoming so cold, hungry, and frightened that they wanted to go back to the place they had escaped. However, she knew that a person returning to slavery would be able to identify members of the Underground Railroad, so she never permitted anyone to go back. Sometimes, she even pointed her Colt revolver at the head of someone who had lost his nerve and said, "Dead [men] tell no tales; you go on or you die!" They went on.[122]

Husbands and Wives

• Kermit Roosevelt used to tell a story about his famous father, Theodore, who was friends with Quanah Parker, chief of the Comanches. Chief Parker had adopted many of the ways of the white man but still was a polygamist with many wives. Mr. Roosevelt asked him why he didn't choose one woman to be his wife and simply pay the living expenses of the others without living with them, pointing out that he could be faithful to one wife while maintaining the other four women. Chief Parker answered that he would do as Mr. Roosevelt asked — with this condition: "You pick out the one I am to retain, and then go tell the other four."[123]

• When Laura Ingalls married Almanzo Wilder on 25 August 1885, she talked to the preacher, Reverend Brown, ahead of time. As she requested, he did not use the word "obey" in the wedding vows.

Later, Laura Ingalls Wilder became famous as the author of the *Little House* books, including *Little House on the Prairie* and *Little House in the Big Woods*.[124]

• Escape artist Harry Houdini's wife, Bess, tried to take good care of her husband, but she didn't always succeed. Once, when he was going on tour for a week, she packed a week's worth of shirts for him, but when he returned, she discovered that he had worn one shirt for the entire week — the others had never even been unpacked.[125]

• One preacher's wife is keenly aware of her most embarrassing moment. During one of her husband's sermons, she fell asleep, her head fell back, her mouth fell open, and her jaw locked into place. Her husband had to stop preaching so he could help her get her mouth closed again.[126]

Language

• Joe S. Warlick was a Church of Christ preacher at a time when Church of Christ preachers were not popular. At a meeting, he had the audience write down questions, which he then read out loud and answered to the best of his ability. One of the questions was, "What's the difference between a Church of Christ preacher and a jackass?" Preacher Warlick read that question out loud, then said, "If whoever wrote this question will come up here and stand by me, I'll show you the difference." And when Mr. Warlick was debating a Baptist preacher in the days when there was a great deal of hostility between these groups, the Baptist preacher called Mr. Warlick a "long-horned ox from Texas." Mr. Warlick replied that in that case the congregation had sinned, because the Bible had orders not to yoke together an ox and an ass. By the way, long ago, Church of Christ preacher J.D. Tant got in trouble for using the word "bull" in a sermon. The congregation thought that the word was indelicate for a woman's ears and preferred the use of "Mr. Cow."[127]

• Benjamin Franklin used to tell a story about a hatter who wished to open a shop. He designed a sign that would display the picture of a hat and these words: "John Thompson, Hatter, makes and sells hats for ready money." He then showed the design for the sign to his friends. The first friend objected to the word "Hatter" because the sign already had the words "makes hats," so "Hatter" was deleted. The second friend said the word "makes" wasn't needed because as long as the hats were well made, people would not care who had made them. The third friend said the words "for ready money" weren't needed because people expected to pay cash for their purchases (this was long before credit cards). The next friend said "sells" was unneeded, as no one expected the store to give them away; in addition, the word "hats" was unneeded because the sign had the picture of a hat on it. When the sign was created, it had on it only the words "John Thompson" and the picture of a hat.[128]

• Jeanie Burt, a nurse at Searcy, Arkansas, knows a colleague who tells about a woman who had had a lot of children, and who asked about using contraception. Nursing staff taught her about using a diaphragm and told her to insert it at night in case of intimacy. Six weeks later, the woman was pregnant although she insisted that she had inserted the diaphragm every night. It turned out that her husband worked at night and was home during the day. Nurse Burt says that this anecdote underscores "the importance of a thorough history and very careful word selection."[129]

• On a live broadcast of a TV show titled *Central Florida Showcase*, the inventor of Gatorade, Dr. Robert Cade, was interviewed. After being asked what the original drink tasted like, Dr. Cade said, "The first Gatorade was served to a football team. A player got it. He was a guard ... who plays for the Steelers now. He got the first drink of Gatorade, took a big swallow, and said, 'This stuff tastes like p*ss.'"[130]

• Rose, the daughter of Laura Ingalls Wilder, author of *Little House on the Prairie*, was bored while attending the third grade, so she developed her own language. It had all the regular parts of speech, such as verbs and nouns, and she called it Fispooko. The language was not wasted — she spoke it to her donkey, whose name was Spookendyke. As an adult, Rose became a well-known author.[131]

• Amy Tan, author of *The Joy Luck Club*, published an early story titled "Rules of the Game" in *Seventeen*. Later, a friend called to congratulate her for having the story translated into Italian and published in an Italian magazine. This shocked Ms. Tan, as she had not given her permission for this to happen. Because of this experience, she decided she needed an agent.[132]

• Charles Nolan, Andrew Tobias' significant other, threw him a surprise 50th birthday party. Despite having been looked at by several people, the invitation said, "SUPRISE!" When Mr. Tobias threw a surprise 40th birthday party for Mr. Nolan a few weeks later, he made sure the invitation said, "SURRPRISE!"[133]

• Sydney Smith, a master of puns, was once forced to turn down a social invitation: "Dear Longman, I can't accept your invitation, for my house is full of country cousins. I wish they were once removed."[134]

• Yogi Berra once arrived five minutes late for a radio interview. Because he was usually 30 minutes late for interviews, he remarked, "I guess this is the earliest I've ever been late."[135]

Mindless Consumption

• All of us should resist mindless consumption. Sometimes, something good is changed into something that is mindless consumption. For example, the riot grrrl movement believed (and believes) in Revolution Girl Style Now! The pop group Spice Girls co-opted this good thing and changed it to "Girl Power," which sounds good. However, what does "Girl Power" mean? The Spice Girls sold a lot of products. On those products appeared such messages as this: "Thank you for making us the number one act in the world. And thanks for buying this officially licensed product. Girl Power forever!" A cynic could say that the phrase "Girl Power" means to spend one's money to enhance the popularity and wealth of the Spice Girls. In contrast, the phrase "Revolution Girl Style Now!" means to work toward a better world for all girls and women — which actually would also be a better world for all boys and men. Too much attention is placed on products that say, "I'm a fan of this band." Not enough attention is placed on messages that say, "I'm a revolutionary feminist, and I won't rest until sexism is obliterated," in words that appear in Sara Marcus' *Girls to the Front*.[136]

• In the early days of television, TVs were expensive and having a TV was a status symbol. Quite a few houses had TV antennas prominently displayed outside — but no TV inside.[137]

Mishaps

• Actor Sheldon Leonard once had a mother's helper who acquired a severe case of head lice. She was too embarrassed to get her prescription filled at a pharmacy, so Mr. Leonard did it for her. He had just handed the prescription to the pharmacist when his co-star, the beautiful actress Hedy Lamarr, walked up behind him. At just that moment, the pharmacist said, "Somebody's got a bad case of lice." Mr. Leonard writes in his autobiography, *And the Show Goes On*, that Ms. Lamarr avoided him for the rest of the filming of the movie they made together.[138]

• In the early days of television, technical directors worked long hours. After working 30 hours in a row — with no sleep — on the *Colgate Comedy Hour*, Bob Finch collapsed during its live performance. The producer, worried about keeping the show on the air, yelled, "Somebody get an ambulance — but first, get me a replacement for Finch." By the way, Red Skelton once got stuck in an elevator in his TV studio with no means of communicating with anybody. Because Mr. Skelton was a big star, a red telephone was immediately installed in that particular elevator.[139]

• During war, supplies are limited, and so governments must make decisions about where cutbacks can be made in order to divert material to the use of the military. During World War II, the United States War Production Board decided to phase out the manufacture of alarm clocks, but when workers began to arrive late for their shifts in factories manufacturing much-needed materials, it realized that it had made a mistake and authorized their production once more.[140]

• On the old TV show *What's My Line*, the panelists would try to guess the unusual occupation of the contestant. Once, the contestant was a mattress stuffer, and a panelist asked, "Is your product used by one sex over the other?"[141]

Money

• Pope John XXIII was a humble man and disliked being carried in the *Sedia Gestatoria*, the sedan chair with which several men carried the Pope through great public gatherings. There was another reason the Holy Father disliked the *Sedia Gestatoria*. After making one of his first trips in it, he got down and said, "The motion of that rocking chair makes me dizzy." Soon after his election, Pope John XXIII, who was a heavy man, inquired about the wages of the men who carried the *Sedia Gestatoria*. When asked why he was concerned about such a small matter, he replied, "They should receive a bonus to compensate them for the increase in papal weight."[142]

• Herbert Hoover traveled frequently by boat between London and Belgium during World War I, because he was in charge of the Belgian relief work. The trip took a full day, and it was his custom to pay for all of his three meals at the end of the trip, rather than to pay for each meal separately. The boats were very small, and they were not targets of warfare; however, mines in the water were dangerous. One day, Mr. Hoover ate breakfast and then told the steward that he would pay at the end of the day as usual, but the steward told him, "I'm sorry, sir, but when the last boat was blown up the passengers got drowned. We may be sunk at any moment, so I must collect cash after each meal."[143]

• Abraham was known for his generosity to strangers. He often fed travelers and when they offered to pay him, he would reply, "Keep your money, for God will pay me." One day, King Nimrod, who forced his countrymen to call him a god, decided to visit Abraham. He and all his warriors took advantage of all Abraham's hospitality. However, King Nimrod was surprised when, after the visit was over, Abraham presented him with a bill. "I thought that you always say that God will repay you," King Nimrod said. "That is true," said Abraham, "but you say that you are God."[144]

• A man arrived at the Pearly Gates, but he discovered that Heaven was so full that no more people could enter. However, St. Peter told him that he could enter under one condition. He would be allowed to send in a note to the inhabitants of Heaven, and if an inhabitant voluntarily left Heaven, the man could take his place. The man quickly scribbled a few words on a piece of paper, then St. Peter sent the note in to Heaven. Very quickly, people stampeded for the gates and almost everyone in Heaven left. Curious, St. Peter asked, "What did you write on the note?" The man replied, "I wrote, 'Gold has been discovered in Hell.'"[145]

• Many celebrities were seriously hurt financially by the 1929 stock market crash — among them, Groucho Marx. Groucho had been encouraged to invest in the stock market by fellow comedian Eddie Cantor, who also lost a fortune and who felt bad because of his advice to Groucho. After the crash, Mr. Cantor asked Groucho how he was feeling, and Groucho replied, "I feel so low, Eddie, I could walk, with a high hat, under a duck without touching him." By the way, a woman once walked up to Groucho Marx and asked, "Aren't you Groucho Marx?" "No," Groucho answered. "Are you?"[146]

• In Pittsburgh, the restaurant called Captain Cook's was owned by Barney Cook, who liked to joke with his customers. One customer, Joe the letter carrier, became very ill in the restaurant. His face was pale, he was breathing with great effort, his face was turning blue, and of course an ambulance was called immediately. Mr. Cook leaned down over Joe and asked, "Joe, can you hear me?" Joe weakly replied that he could. Mr. Cook then asked, "Have you paid your check?" Joe began to laugh, his color returned, and he was in much better shape by the time the ambulance arrived.[147]

• A miser once dug a hole in his backyard, and hid all his money in it instead of buying the necessities of life for his family. One day, his son discovered the hiding place of the money, and he took all the gold out of the hole and dropped a large stone in the hole to take the place of the money. Then the son took the money and spent it on food, shelter, and clothing for the family. When the miser discovered the stone in the hiding place, he was very sad, but his son told him, "Money is for spending; if you wish to hide something, hide a stone."[148]

• Mark Twain once told a story that illustrated why speakers should be brief: Mr. Twain said he attended a church when a missionary began to speak. At first Mr. Twain was fired up with enthusiasm for the missionary's work and wanted to donate the $400 he had and borrow all he could to give to the missionary. However, the missionary kept talking, and the longer the missionary talked, the less enthusiastic Mr. Twain became — when the offering plate was finally passed around, Mr. Twain stole ten cents from it.[149]

• John Waters is a trial junkie, and he enjoys watching the trials of famous criminals. Sometimes, he even visits the criminals in prison and becomes friends with them. He even befriended Charles "Tex" Watson, who was the lieutenant of the infamous gang of murderers led by Charles Manson. Once, they got to talking about what Tex should do if he were ever released from prison, and Mr. Waters told him he should become "the highest-paid bill collector in America."[150]

• Pepsi spends a fortune on its TV commercials; production costs for some of the commercials are more than $1 million each. In fact, at Pepsi, people joked that they gave their ad agency, BBDO, an unlimited budget, but that BBDO managed to exceed it. By the way,

BBDO created the commercial titled "Archeologist," in which a Pepsi-drinking archeologist of the future is unable to identify a Coke bottle.[151]

• Martin Luther King, Jr., was assassinated on 4 April 1968. Despite the huge amount of good he did during his 39 years of life, he was never a rich man. Dr. King made $6,000 per year as co-pastor of Ebenezer Baptist Church in Atlanta, Georgia. When he died, he left behind a $50,000 insurance policy and almost $5,000 in the bank.[152]

• Early in her career, Betty White was asked to do the first TV commercial for a feminine hygiene product. The manufacturers were hoping that the country would accept such a commercial if Ms. White were selling the product. However, Ms. White firmly replied that there wasn't enough money in the world to tempt her into doing a commercial for that particular product.[153]

• A poor man told a miser that he and the miser were equal in wealth. The miser expressed amazement, but the poor man pointed out that he could not spend money because he was poor, while the miser did not spend money because he was a miser. They spent the same amount of money, and therefore they were equal in wealth.[154]

• While in Russia in the days when the Soviet Union still existed, actor Robert Morley was given a ticket for jaywalking. The police officer who gave him the ticket also gave him a receipt for the amount of the fine, saying it was "a souvenir of our dreaded secret police."[155]

• Jennifer Camper is a lesbian cartoonist whose cartoons sometimes make men think that she is a dominatrix. Occasionally, these men call her to set up a date, but since she is not a dominatrix, she tells them that they can't afford her prices.[156]

Chapter 4: From Mothers to Problem-Solving

Mothers

• Francis Hodgson Burnett, author of *A Little Princess* and *The Secret Garden*, gave birth to two boys: Lionel and Vivian. When Vivian was born, her older son, Lionel, was jealous and suggested that the new baby be thrown into the fire. By the way, she used to tell her two young sons "hair-curling stories." These weren't stories that frightened the two boys — they were stories to keep the boys quiet and still so she could curl their hair.[157]

• When Joseph Epstein was a small boy of six or seven, he was bored, and he whined to his mother about being bored. She replied, "Really? May I suggest that you knock your head against the wall. It'll take your mind off your boredom." Mr. Epstein writes, "I never again told my mother that I was bored."[158]

• The mother of celebrated African-American writer Toni Cade Bambara believed in education, and she made several unannounced visits to the schools her children attended so she could inspect the schools and make sure they were competent. She also insisted that black history be taught to her children.[159]

Movies

• In the early days of motion pictures, Jim Cruze received a salary of $7,001 per week to direct the movie *The Covered Wagon* for Jesse Lasky because he said he wanted more than $1,000 per day. By the way, Mr. Cruze didn't like the idea of men giving up their seats for healthy women: "If she's a strong enough lady, she can find a seat for herself." Also by the way, Mr. Cruze used to employ many African-American servants back in the days of Jim Crow, and he cautioned visitors to his house not to say anything racial: "It's bad enough to have to work for me. No use to go out of our way to hurt their feelings."[160]

• On 1 May 1930, famous union organizer Mother Jones celebrated her 100th birthday. Friends and reporters surrounded her at her party, and the event was even filmed by movie cameras — Mother Jones was excited to be part of a movie with sound. But when the cameraman tried to explain to her how to speak for the camera, she snapped, "What the hell do you know about it? I was making speeches before you were born!"[161]

• When Mae West was asked about the character she played in the movie *I'm No Angel*, she replied, "I wrote the story myself. It's all about a girl who lost her reputation but never missed it. She's the kind of girl who climbed the ladder of success, wrong by wrong."[162]

Music

• When she was 18, Ethel Merman first starred on Broadway in a musical by George Gershwin. Mr. Gershwin invited Ms. Merman to his penthouse, where he played the two songs she was to sing in *Girl Crazy*. After hearing the songs, Ms. Merman sat quietly, thinking about how she would phrase the lyrics while singing. Mr. Gershwin joked, "Miss Merman, if there's anything about these songs you don't like, I'd be happy to make any changes." The 18-year-old unknown replied, "I think these'll do very nicely, George." (One of the songs was the hit "I Got Rhythm.")[163]

• Leo Slezak was one of the world's great tenors, and so he was a celebrity in any country that loved opera. Of course, being a celebrity does have advantages. Once he took his children to an amusement park, where he decided to shoot an air rifle at a target. The proprietor recognized him, casually asked what target he was shooting at, then said in a voice loud enough to reach the back of the tent, "Ah, the tiger." Mr. Slezak then aimed at a different target, fired the rifle, the tiger fell down, and he won a prize.[164]

• When some new officers presented themselves to the Duke of Wellington, he looked them over, then said, "I don't know what effect they will have upon the enemy, but by God, they frighten me!" By the way, Wellington was once asked if Beethoven's composition titled *Battle of Vitoria* resembled the battle. He replied, "By God, no. If it had, I should have run away myself."[165]

• Maria Callas once sang in *Norma* in Paris, but unfortunately her voice broke on a note, with the result that the audience booed her. She held up her hand for silence, asked the conductor to start the aria from the beginning, and this time reached the note — to the very great applause of the audience.[166]

• Julie Budd was a young singer who appeared many times on *The Merv Griffin Show* in the days before he originated the popular game show *Wheel of Fortune*. Once, the audience started laughing after Mr. Griffin said, "Since we discovered Julie when she was 12, she really developed."[167]

• In England, a song about Mae West was titled "If Those Hips Could Only Speak." When Ms. West heard about the song, she commented, "What do they mean 'if they could only speak'? I can make mine talk anytime."[168]

Names

• When Elwyn Brooks White, who is better known as E.B. White, author of *Charlotte's Web*, attended Cornell University, its president was Andrew White. As a show of affection, Cornell students gave the nickname "Andy" to any student whose last name was "White." The nickname stayed with E.B. White throughout his life. By the way, even as a child, Elwyn wanted to be a writer. He used to read *St. Nicholas* magazine, which encouraged children to send in writing and puzzles, and so Elwyn sent in a story. St. Nicholas published it, and Elwyn was proud — even though the magazine misspelled his name as "Elwin."[169]

• Vicki Crooks' four-year-old son asked her about God's name, so she explained that God has many names, and he answers to all of them: Father, Jehovah, Lord, etc. Her son asked, "Can I just call him Steve?"[170]

Old Age

• In November 2003, a 92-year-old Sikh man named Fauja Singh wore a turban as he completed the New York City Marathon (26.2 miles) in 7½ hours. (Of course, this is a slow pace. Many young, healthy people can walk four miles in one hour.) His reason for participating in the marathon was to bring attention to his religion, which in the 1500s was founded in Punjab, India. Mr. Singh, a British citizen, said, "Sikhs are not a part of any other religion. It is its own religion." He endured taunts by bystanders who called him such names as "Osama Bin Laden" as he participated in the marathon, but he said, "I wasn't hurt by it. Those comments had nothing to do with the race." Many other people cheered for him rather than taunted him. In addition to participating in the marathon, Mr. Singh won the Ellis Island Medal of Honor, which the National Ethnic Coalition Organization awarded him. This group promotes ethnic pride and ethnic tolerance. William Fugazy, the chairman of the coalition, said about Mr. Singh, "He is the greatest inspiration." Mr. Singh is the first non-American to be given the Ellis Island Medal of Honor. Mr. Singh's ability to complete a marathon of 26.2 miles at age 92 is remarkable. He said, "Other people my age are hobbling around with sticks. I am blessed with the ability to do this." Mr. Singh participated in his first marathon at age 86. His personal best time is 5 hours, 40 minutes, which he achieved in the Waterfront Marathon at Toronto. Mr. Singh said, "I actually owe it to the grace of God to allow me to do such things." Mr. Singh visited Central Park before participating in the marathon. He said, "It's a lovely place. But lovely places are only lovely because of the people."[171]

• Catherine Shipley was both a Quaker and a character. When she was old and living alone, her children became worried about her, so they hired a companion for her. Knowing that Kate didn't want a companion, they told the companion not to leave Kate's home, even when requested to do so. The companion arrived at Kate's home and was entertained, and she did not leave even when Kate requested her to once, twice, and three times. However, Kate was master of her own home, and she called the police, who carried the companion off to jail.[172]

• According to Sir Rudolf Bing, Mary Garden came to his box at the Metropolitan Opera wearing a low-cut, strapless dress, although she was then an old lady. An even older man asked her, "What makes that dress stay up?" She replied, "Your age, sir."[173]

• Chief Justice of the Supreme Court Oliver Wendell Holmes, age 80, was walking with a friend when, in front of them, the wind flipped up the skirt of a pretty, young woman. Chief Justice Holmes sighed, "Oh, to be 70 again."[174]

Parents

• At age 16, Anissa Ayala began to suffer from lumps on her ankles and severe pains in her stomach. Her parents, Abe and Mary Ayala, took her to a doctor and discovered that she was suffering from a rare form of leukemia. Worse, she needed rounds of radiation and chemotherapy — and a bone marrow transplant. Without a bone marrow transplant, she would die. Her parents were tested to see if they could be donors, but they were not good donors for their daughter. Neither was her brother. In desperation, Abe and Mary Ayala decided to conceive a child who might be a bone-marrow donor. Mary was 42, an age that reduced her chances of having a successful pregnancy, and Abe had to get a vasectomy reversed. In addition, the baby had only a 23 percent chance of being a successful donor. However, their plan worked. Baby Marissa was born in April 1990, and when she was 14 months old some of her bone marrow was put into her sister's body. In 2011, 20 years later, Anissa's body was still free of cancer. The Ayalas' decision to have a baby to serve as a donor of bone marrow was heavily criticized at the time, but in 2011 Marissa, a senior in college, said, "People are entitled to their own opinions, but I am so glad that I am in this family. I could not have asked for a better family, so I've never questioned it." One critic at first was medical correspondent Dr. Nancy

Snyderman, who in 2011 said about the Ayala's decision, "It crossed so many medical ethical lines. I remember thinking early on, I was very critical of this, as a doctor. Then I thought, 'Well, as a mother, would I do it?' And then I thought, 'Yes, I would.'" Marissa said about Anissa, "Without her and her sickness, I would not be here. And without me being a perfect match for my sister, she would not be here as well."[175]

• As a child, author Saul Bellow nearly died from a bout with peritonitis in the days before antibiotics. In fact, he was so ill that his parents changed his first name — an old Jewish custom that is followed in an effort to hide the seriously ill child from Death.[176]

Parties

• Franklin Pierce Adams, George Kaufman, and Beatrice Kaufman (Mrs. George Kaufman) once attended a cocktail party. Mrs. Kaufman had the misfortune to sit on a poorly made cane-bottom chair. The cane-bottom broke, Mrs. Kaufman's bottom fell, and she was stuck in the chair's frame. Mr. Adams merely looked at her and said, "I've told you a hundred times, Beatrice — that's not funny."[177]

• When Dr. Martin Luther King, Jr., received the 1964 Nobel Peace Prize, not everyone was happy. In January 1965, as Dr. King attended a reception in his honor at the Dinkler Hotel in Atlanta, Georgia, troops of hooded Ku Klux Klansmen marched outside the hotel. Inside the hotel, blacks and whites enjoyed a nice party.[178]

Pleasing Everyone

• Nasrudin and his son were going to market with their donkey. As Nasrudin led the donkey, his son rode on the donkey's back. They met a man who said, "Look at the boy riding the donkey! He ought to show respect for his father by letting the father ride on the donkey's back." So the son got off the donkey's back and allowed Nasrudin to ride the donkey. Next they met a man who said to Nasrudin, "Your son is too young to walk such a long distance. He, not you, should be riding the donkey." So Nasrudin allowed his son to ride the donkey with him. Next they met a man who said, "You are mistreating that poor donkey by making him carry the two of you. You two should get off the donkey and let him rest." Next they met a man who said, "Why are you two walking beside your donkey? You have a donkey, so why don't at least one of you ride him?" On hearing this, Nasrudin thought, "It's true — you can't please everyone."[179]

• Buddhist meditation halls have an image of the Buddha, and meditators traditionally bow to the Buddha when they enter the meditation hall. This is the practice of meditation teacher Sharon Salzberg, who once received two notes after bowing to the Buddha. The first note said, "I saw you bowing to the Buddha, and I was really offended. It is rank superstition, and it has no place here. You should stop doing it. The second note said, "I saw you bowing to the Buddha, and I want you to know that it was the most moving thing that has ever happened to me here. It made all the difference in my retreat. I am so grateful that you did it."[180]

Politics

• Back when Joe McCarthy was making it hot for anyone who believed in the Constitution and the Bill of Rights, Texas legislator Maury Maverick, Jr., stood up in the Texas House of Representatives and read these words: "All political power is inherent in the people, and all free governments are founded on their authority, and instituted for their benefit. The faith of the people of Texas stands pledged to the preservation of a republican form of government, and subject to this limitation only, they have at all times the inalienable right to alter, reform, or abolish their government in such manner as they think expedient." Immediately, Mr. Maverick was accused of reading seditious words and it was demanded that he give an apology. Finally, someone thought to ask where the words Mr. Maverick had read had come from: They were from the Constitution of the State of Texas.[181]

• During the Civil Rights movement, police officers used German shepherds to attack activists who were trying to register African Americans so they could vote. In 1963, as Marian Wright Edelman was trying to register blacks in Greenwood, Mississippi, German shepherds controlled by the police attacked her, although Federal Bureau of Investigation agents were standing nearby. Nearly 40 years after the dogs attacked her, she still crosses the street whenever she sees a German shepherd. Ms. Edelman is a strong advocate of voting and points out that if you vote, you can elect politicians who will protect civil rights and won't allow the police to use dogs to attack law-abiding people, including children.[182]

• A man once insulted Benjamin Disraeli by saying that his wife had picked him out of the gutter. Mr. Disraeli responded, "My good fellow, if you were in the gutter no one would pick you out." By the way, asked to explain the difference between "misfortune:" and "calamity," Mr. Disraeli made a joke about his political rival, William Gladstone: "If Mr. Gladstone fell into the Thames, it would be a misfortune, but if someone pulled him out, it would be a calamity." And near the end of his life, Mr. Disraeli proofread a copy of his final speech in Parliament, saying, "I will not go down to posterity speaking bad grammar."[183]

Practical Jokes

• During World War II, some of Walter Winchell's friends pulled a practical joke on him. Immediately following his radio broadcast, Mr. Winchell was handed a telegram that said: "The Berlin radio reports that Adolf Hitler has been killed while inspecting Eastern Front defenses." Mr. Winchell screamed, "Damn the luck! Hitler's dead and I'm off the air!" However, after learning that the telegram was a fake, he said, "I'd go off the air forever if no more bombs were dropped on babies, if no more people were shot because they believed in something different, if there would be no more prejudice with a gun in its hand."[184]

• Opera singer Leo Slezak's mother-in-law was a beautiful woman with two sons and two daughters. One day, she and her daughters were beautifully dressed and riding in their carriage at a big social event, throwing flowers to the crowds watching them. Suddenly, her two sons, who had dressed themselves as filthy street urchins, came up to the carriage and yelled, "Mama, Mama, we want to ride in the parade with you." Of course, the crowd enjoyed the scene, but she was furious at being made the laughing-stock of Vienna.[185]

• In his book *The Compleat Practical Joker*, H. Allen Smith tells about Brian G. Hughes, a manufacturer in Manhattan who used to go into a bar on a rainy day and purposely leave his umbrella at the bar so it would be stolen. Then he would find himself a good seat and wait for the thief to go out into the rain and open the umbrella — from which would fall confetti and streamers reading "This umbrella stolen from Brian G. Hughes."[186]

Prayer

• Abdul Qadir al-Jilani was still asleep as the time of his morning prayer neared. However, a cat came by and brushed against him, waking him in time for the prayer. After his morning prayer was over, al-Jilani looked carefully at the cat and saw that it was not a cat at all, but a devil in the form of a cat. So al-Jilani asked the devil-cat, "Since you are a devil, why did you wake me in time for my morning prayer?" The devil-cat answered, "Since you have seen through my disguise, I will tell you. I know your character. If you had missed your morning prayer, you would have said 100 prayers to make up for the one prayer you missed. I woke you so you would get credit only for the one prayer — not for the 100 prayers you would have said."[187]

• The Baal Shem Tov believed in the prayers of women. He told a story about a community of Jews who were worried about a great calamity. They gathered at the Ark of the Covenant and prayed, but Heaven remained unmoved and unmerciful until a woman prayed, "Master of the Universe! Thou art a merciful Father. Thy children are pouring out their hearts to Thee. I am a mother of five children and when I hear their cry, my heart goes out to them. Heavenly Father, Thou hast many children. Even if Thy heart were made of stone, it should melt at the agonizing cry of Thy children. O God, listen to them and save them."[188]

• An atheist was observed praying on Yom Kippur. When he was asked why he was praying, the atheist replied, "You know that I am a doubter. Well, as a doubter, I also have doubts about atheism."[189]

Problem-Solving

• As a graffiti artist, Banksy does illegal things, meaning that he has to work fast and avoid the authorities. When he was 18, he tried to paint "LATE AGAIN" on the side of a passenger train, but in the midst of his painting the British transport police arrived and he had to run and hide under the bottom of a fuel tank. He realized that he needed to paint much faster to avoid being arrested. As he thought this, he looked up at the bottom of the fuel tank and saw some stencilled information. Banksy says, "I realized that I could just copy that style and make each letter three feet high." He then went home and told his girlfriend that he had had an epiphany that night. She misunderstood and told him not to take that drug because it is bad for your heart. As a satirist, Banksy is aware that many Americans are fat. In fact, he jokes, "A recent survey of North American males found 42% were overweight, 34% were critically obese and 8% ate the survey." Some North American cities have bike lanes for bicyclists; in a satiric act, Banksy used stencils to create a "FAT LANE." Among Banksy's beliefs are "Nothing in the world is more common than unsuccessful people with talent" and "Artwork that is only about wanting to be famous will never make you famous. Fame is a by-product of doing something else. You don't go to a restaurant and order a meal because you want to have a sh*t."[190]

• Edgar White, a reporter, was once asked to interview Mark Twain on a certain subject. He went to Mr. Twain's hotel close to midnight, and was shown to Mr. Twain's room. Mr. Twain was in bed, reading and smoking. Unfortunately, Mr. Twain announced that he couldn't talk about the reporter's proposed topic, as a contract he had signed forbade it. Mr. White was understandably disappointed and said in that case he had nothing to write about. "I've been in that fix many and many a time," Mr. Twain said. "Now if I were the reporter and you were the man in bed I'd tell how, over the vigorous remonstrances of the clerk I'd come up here in the dead hour of the night and aroused you from a sound sleep to ...." Mr. White interrupted to point out that that was not the truth — the clerk had politely shown him to the room and Mr. Twain had not been asleep. Mr. Twain sighed, then said, "If you're going to let a little thing like that stand in the way, I'm afraid I can't help you. Good night." Mr. White decided to write an article stating the absolute truth, just as it is related here. The newspaper ran his article under a big headline.[191]

• A group devoted to meditation used to rent sites for its retreats before establishing the Insight Meditation Society in Barre, Massachusetts. One of the retreats was held in a monastery with a chapel; to convert the chapel into a meditation hall, the pews of the chapel were stored in a back room. One of the meditators, who was staying in the back room because of a lack of sleeping space, began to suffer from discomfort during the meditation sessions, so he sat in one of the pews and began to design the perfect meditation chair. As he designed the chair, he felt happier and happier. At first, he thought he was happy because he was designing the perfect meditation chair, then he realized that he was happy because he was so comfortable. He looked around and saw that there were about 300 pews in the back room; what he had been looking for was right in front of him.[192]

• It pays to have a script supervisor on a television series. At a story conference for the episode "The Twizzle" on *The Dick Van Dyke Show*, the principals of the show were having a hard time figuring out what was wrong with a scene, so they met in the commissary later, came up with several ideas, and figured out how to fix it. Series creator Carl Reiner then asked, "My God, is anybody getting this down?" Fortunately, script supervisor Marge Mullen wrote the ideas down on a napkin, then typed them up later. Ms. Mullen also came up with the idea of the "SOS" ("Some Other Show") notebook. Often, people would have good ideas for the series, but they wouldn't fit the particular episode being worked on. Ms. Mullen wrote down the ideas and kept them in her SOS notebook. When people became stuck for ideas, she used the SOS notebook as a source of ideas.[193]

• Lindley Miller Garrison served as Secretary of War under President Woodrow Wilson. Much of the reading he had to do while in office was dry and boring, but once he came across something interesting. A colonel had ordered a lieutenant to take 15 men across a swamp, but although the lieutenant was a capable man, he did not want to do so, arguing that the mud was too deep. However, under orders he made the attempt, but returned with himself and his men covered with mud. The lieutenant told his colonel, "Sir, the mud is over my men's heads. I cannot do it." The colonel then ordered the lieutenant to requisition anything that was needed for him to take 15 men across the swamp, so the lieutenant filled out the necessary requisition form: "I want fifteen men eighteen feet long to cross a swamp fifteen feet deep."[194]

• A student in the old Orient was learning about tricks that are used in war. For example, the student learned of an army that was in a weak position. To keep from being attacked at night, the general ordered many more fires to be built than were actually needed. This made his army appear to be stronger than it really was. Another example: A general had a strong army, but he wished to keep the number of soldiers secret from the enemy. Therefore, he ordered many fewer fires to be built than usual. This made his army appear to be weaker than it really was. The student disliked this trickery and told his teacher, "I am an honorable man, and when I am a general, I won't use tricks." The teacher told the student that a special place existed for generals like him: the graveyard.[195]

• Some incredible stories about Japanese ninjas have been told. A ninja was once being chased by guards, but he escaped by using a hidden springboard to jump over a 10-foot wall. The guards chasing the ninja didn't see the springboard, so they thought the ninja had managed to jump a superhuman height. By the way, the Japanese ninjas were masters of camouflage, which they learned as the art of invisibility. While working at night, they wore black clothing. While working among rocks, they wore grey clothing. While working in snow, they wore white clothing. While working in a forest, they wore green clothing. Often, the clothing they wore was reversible, so they could switch to another color if needed.[196]

• Lots of people Google their own names. Alec Brownstein did that, too, and he noticed that when he Googled his name that no ads came up. He had the goal of working for one of the top advertising agencies in New York City, and so he spent $6 on ads that would be triggered when five of the creative directors of the top advertising agencies in New York City searched for their own names. One ad said, "Hey, Ian Reichenthal, Gooogling [sic] yourself is a lot of fun. Hiring me is fun, too." Mr. Brownstein targeted five creative directors and ended up with four interviews and two job offers, including one from Mr. Reichenthal. Very impressive, especially considering that he misspelled "Googling."[197]

• Hershel Ostropoler arrived at an inn late one evening and asked for food, but the proprietor of the inn looked at him, realized that he was poor, and said that no more food was left. Hearing that, Mr. Ostropoler hit the table with his fist, then shouted with an angry voice, "I have no choice! I must do what my father did!" The proprietor became afraid and quickly ordered food to be brought to Mr. Ostropoler. After he had eaten, the proprietor asked what his father had done. Mr. Ostropoler replied, "Whenever my beloved father could find no dinner, he went to bed hungry."[198]

• Rosanna Gartley, a nurse in McKees Rocks, PA, had an elderly patient who was a problem-solver. He needed foot care, which normally required a 10-minute pre-soak. However, he showed up wearing shorts and rubber boots and said that he didn't have time for a pre-soak: "I've got things to do." He had gotten up early, put on rubber boots and filled them with water, and then gone about his daily routine, which included gardening and having coffee with friends. Ms. Gartley writes, "He had the cleanest, most shriveled feet I have ever seen!"[199]

• Sir Rudolf Bing once had a problem when Birgit Nilsson made a huge success in *Tristan und Isolde*. Unfortunately, the three singers who could play Tristan to her Isolde fell ill. However, Sir Rudolf solved the problem when he discovered that although none of the male singers were well enough to perform the entire opera, each of them could perform one act. The audience laughed when they heard Sir Rudolf's announcement about the three Tristans they would see in one performance, and the performance was a success.[200]

• Quakers tend to try to avoid pride of ownership of material possessions, especially during meetings. Benjamin Maule (1794-1873) was especially proud of a horse that he often rode to meetings. However, some Quakers noticed that he had not ridden the horse to meetings in a few weeks, and Mr. Maule confessed to selling the horse. When they expressed surprise that he would sell a horse he was so obviously proud of, Mr. Maule replied, "I felt I should; he would [figuratively] come into meeting with me."[201]

• In *The Avengers*, John Steed drove a vintage Bentley, even though off screen the Bentleys used in the TV series seldom worked correctly. Often, to get a vintage Bentley started, it had to be pushed down a hill. Often, the car couldn't get out of third gear. Sometimes, the car was even pushed into view by studio technicians, and the film was speeded up later to make it look like the Bentley was going at a decent speed.[202]

• Cynthia Kahn owned a small sweets shop that competed with a store in a national chain. In fact, she was winning the competition. Reporters asked her for the secret of her success, and she explained, "In the other store, when customers order a pound of candy, the salesgirls scoop up more than a pound of candy, then they start taking away. In my store, I scoop up less than a pound of candy, then start adding."[203]

• Zen master Hakuju was lecturing at the Tendai Sect College on a very hot day when he noticed a couple of students dozing. He said, "It is hot, isn't it? Can't blame you for going to sleep. Mind if I join you?" Hakuju then went to sleep, and his snoring awoke the dozing students, who waited with the other students for him to wake up and resume his lecture.[204]

• Jack Keeshin of Chicago was one of the first truck drivers in the United States — he drove a truck before asphalt was used on the roads. While hauling 18,000 pounds of Fig Newtons, he became stuck in sand. Fortunately, a cemetery was nearby, and he managed to get unstuck and deliver the Fig Newtons by putting 25 gravestones under his truck's wheels.[205]

• Many problems exist in society, but the ingredients for solving those problems also exist in society. Mulla Nasrudin illustrated this when he asked a grocer, "Do you have milk, eggs, flour, sugar, baking soda, butter, and chocolate?" When the grocer said he had all those things, Nasrudin asked, "So why don't you bake some cookies?"[206]

• In Augusta, Georgia, a teacher needed to solve a problem. One of her students was in the nurse's room. He was ill and going home, so he needed his coat. Unfortunately, the teacher didn't know which coat was his. Fortunately, one of her students came up with a solution to the problem: "Let's all put on our coats, and the one that's left will be his."[207]

• The Netherlands were once besieged by the Spanish Duke of Alva during the winter in his attempt to wipe out the Protestants. Because the Dutch fleet was frozen in the harbor, things looked bad for the Netherlands; however, the Dutch soldiers simply grabbed their muskets, put on skates, and skated out to the Spaniards and defeated them.[208]

• Mendele Mocher Seforim (1835-1917) did not like to be disturbed. When a man he disliked wanted to come visit him at home, he would tell the man to knock in a certain way. That way, when the man later knocked on his door, he immediately knew who it was and so he would sit quietly until the man went away.[209]

• Sojourner Truth (1797-1883), a traveling preacher, was a strong African-American woman, and she was dogged by rumors that she was really a man who dressed in women's clothing. Once, she bared one of her breasts before an audience, then said, "It is not my shame, but yours, that I should do this."[210]

• Some restaurants get noisy because of the constant playing of the jukebox. To meet the demand for silence, a record company once produced a record made especially for jukeboxes. When selected, the record plays four minutes of silence.[211]

Chapter 5: From Public Speaking to Work

Public Speaking

• Ben Hecht once went to see a talented fighter named Al Singer, whose opponent was a fighter of little talent named Kid McGirk. During the fight, Mr. Singer kept battering Kid McGirk, but never managed to knock him out. Kid McGirk was clearly outclassed, and the crowd knew it — they kept booing him throughout the fight. After the fight, the referee told the audience that Kid McGirk wanted to speak to them. Kid McGirk began, "Ladies and Gentlemen," and the crowd booed. He continued: "I wanna tell you that I got an announcement to make. That tonight was my last fight." The crowd kept on booing. Kid McGirk then said, "I'm glad you liked my fight tonight b'cuz it's my last fight, see? I've had a wonderful time fighting for you people and I've always appreciated it." As Kid McGirk spoke, the booing slowly diminished in intensity. He then said, "So I wish t' take his occasion t' t'ank you for having been such a fine public and having been so good to me." At this point, the booing had completely stopped. Kid McGirk then ended with, "I have only the memories of the finest time to take back home with me and I want to thank the public for everything they done for me." Now, cheering began. The entire audience began to applaud and cheer for this outclassed fighter whom they had been booing earlier. Al Singer had failed to knock Kid McGirk out, and so had the audience.[212]

• Joseph Hoag of Vermont was a renowned Quaker preacher; his son, Lindley Murray Hoag, also became a renowned Quaker preacher. Mr. Hoag and his son, who was still a young man, attended a Quarterly Meeting where it was expected that the elder Hoag would speak. However, he didn't feel called by the Holy Spirit to speak, so he remained silent. He did, however, feel that his son was remaining silent because his son felt that the people present at the meeting were hoping to hear the elder Hoag speak. To encourage his son to speak, Mr. Hoag nudged his son with his foot, and his son stood up and gave a remarkable sermon. The nudge was seen by the elders of the meeting, who felt that no one should made to speak, but should speak only when moved by the Holy Spirit. Therefore, the elders criticized the elder Mr. Hoag, who responded, "If you can kick a sermon like that out of any of your boys, you had better do it."[213]

• For some people, time flies when they are speaking publicly. The Right Reverend Peter Mumford, Bishop of Truro, once spoke at an important luncheon attended by the Lord Mayor. He was told that the Lord Mayor had to leave promptly for a Royal engagement, and therefore he must not speak past 2:15 p.m. He began speaking at 2:05 p.m., but seemingly very quickly the toastmaster told him that he had to stop although the clock in the room said 2:07 p.m. He protested, "But you said I'd got until quarter past." The toastmaster whispered back, "I know, but the clock stopped."[214]

Religion

• Edwin Porter was a preacher in Texas in the first half of the 20th century. He took his faith seriously. When lightning struck his house one Sunday when he was playing dominoes with some friends, he took it as a sign from God and dumped the dominoes into the fireplace, saying, "Never again shall a domino, deck of cards, or any such appearance of evil enter my house." (Mr. Porter also believed in no shaves and no baths on Sundays; such things had to be taken care of on Saturday before sunset. In addition, he hid the comics from the Sunday newspaper until Monday, when it was proper to read them.)[215]

• One of the rules of Mother Teresa's Missionaries of Charity was that they could accept nothing from the people they served — not even a glass of water. Mother Teresa worried that the poor, out of gratitude, would offer something they could not afford to give away, so she ordered her nuns to accept nothing from the poor. By the way, wherever Mother Teresa went, she gave away small cards with prayers or religious songs printed on them — she joked that they were her business cards.[216]

• Pope John XXIII could be very informal. He once met an ambassador and said, "Your Excellency, let us hand over these formal speeches to our secretaries, and you and I will go to my office and have a quiet talk." By the way, a coat of arms containing a lion was designed for Pope John XXIII, who approved of the overall design for the coat of arms, but did ask for one modification: "Please don't make my lion look so cross."[217]

• Guy D. Mattox, Jr., once received a letter from a woman in his congregation who was away at graduate school. Among other news, the letter stated that she was on a diet and had decided to lose 78 pounds. As a matter of fact, the letter announced, she had already lost 16 pounds. Then she listed a Bible reference — John 6:9. When Mr. Mattox looked it up, he read, "But what are they among so many?"[218]

• Actor Pat O'Brien grew up in Milwaukee, where he remembered a Father Murphy. After one long day, Father Murphy was very tired, and he was faced with a long line of people who wished to go to Confession. He spoke out to the line: "All ye mortals stay, and all ye venials go home!" The church was empty within two minutes. (Mortal sins are much more serious than venial sins.)[219]

• Many people were suspicious of Mother Teresa because they felt that since she was a Catholic nun, she would try to convert them to Christianity. To these people, Mother Teresa said, "I convert you to be a better Hindu, a better Catholic, a better Muslim ... or Buddhist."[220]

Revenge

• Gertrude Stein and Edith Sitwell were sometimes rivals. Ms. Stein once lectured at Oxford, and she embarrassed Ms. Sitwell by ending the lecture with a "word portrait" of her, saying such things as, "Sitwell Edith Sitwell. Introduces have and heard. Miss Edith Sitwell have and heard," and so on. In Paris a few years later, Sylvia Beach asked Ms. Sitwell to lecture on Ms. Stein. At the lecture, for which Ms. Stein was present, Ms. Sitwell recited the work of Shakespeare, other Elizabethans, and herself. During the entire lecture, she mentioned Ms. Stein not once.[221]

• A society editor was once deeply offended by a society woman. To get even, for the next 20 years whenever he wrote an article that mentioned the society woman attending a party, a luncheon, a dinner, the opera, etc., he always described her as wearing exactly the same dress.[222]

Thanksgiving

• At the Web site <Helpothers.org>, a woman named Cecilia wrote about volunteering at a shelter where she and her parents served food to the needy on Thanksgiving. Cecilia was very surprised when a well-groomed man wearing an expensive suit entered the shelter and joined the line for food. She wrote, "The closer he came to my service station, the more I muttered. What was this man doing, I wanted to know? Surely he wasn't going to take food meant for those who were really in need!" Her mother overheard her and said to her, "You have assumed that the needs of the people who come here must be purely physical: hunger, inadequate shelter, clothing, etc. And this gentleman doesn't seem to have any of those problems. But what if his needs are emotional? What if he needs comfort, friends, or just to be amongst other human beings?" Cecilia served the man. About a week later, someone made a large donation to the shelter. Cecilia wrote, "I can't help but wonder if it came from that man? Now, whenever I meet someone I remember my mother's lesson and try to send kindness and blessings their way, regardless of how they look. Needs aren't always visible. But kindness always makes a difference."[223]

• The day before Thanksgiving of 1987, brothers and real estate investors Gil and Troy Gillenwater decided to do something to help other people. They drove to Price Club (which is now Costco), where they bought $2,000 of groceries. They then drove south. Their intention was to go to Nogales, Arizona, but they got lost and ended up in Agua Prieta, Mexico, where they saw an impoverished 22-year-old woman cooking tamales. Playing near the woman were eight children, whom she had started to care for after she found them eating garbage and sleeping in old cars. She lived in a cardboard shack, and she had no electricity and no running water. The Gillenwaters gave away the $2,000 of food, and a few weeks later they returned with materials to build a bathroom for the woman. They kept coming back, and they started the Rancho Feliz Charitable Foundation, which helps impoverished people.[224]

• In 1938, Hattie McDaniel, an African-American actress who would soon win an Academy Award for her performance in *Gone with the Wind*, was happy as she prepared to celebrate Thanksgiving. Things were going well for her, and she was even able to help other people who were less fortunate than she was. In fact, word of her generosity had gotten around. She had planned to celebrate Thanksgiving with only a few guests, but several people whom she had not invited rang her doorbell (her address was in the telephone book) and she welcomed them inside. Fortunately, she had prepared a 20-pound turkey.[225]

Theater

• Actress Sarah Bernhardt was starring in a Paris theater when a boy came to her door to announce that it was eight o'clock and time for her to appear on stage. Because the boy was nervous at being in the presence of such a great star as Ms. Bernhardt, he told her, "Madame, it will be eight o'clock when it suits you." Ms. Bernhardt was so pleased at this remark that she kissed him, and afterwards, at whatever theater she played, it became the custom to announce that it was time for her performance by saying, "Madame, it will be eight o'clock when it suits you."[226]

• Tennessee Williams found it easy to come up with a title for *A Streetcar Named Desire*. He lived in New Orleans, and two streetcars ran past his apartment: one streetcar was named "Desire," and the other was named "Cemeteries." Blanche Du Bois' first line in the play is, "They told me to take a streetcar named Desire, then transfer to one called Cemeteries."[227]

• Richard Brinsley Sheridan scored an immediate success when his comic play *The School for Scandal* was first performed on 8 May 1777. There was so much applause and laughter that a pedestrian walking by the theater thought it was collapsing and fled to safety.[228]

Tobacco

• As a young man, Art Linkletter thought that only English gentlemen and sissies used snuff, so he was surprised when some burly welders he worked with used snuff. They became aware of his thoughts about snuff, and one welder forced him to take off a shoe and a sock. The welder then put some snuff between two of Art's toes and had him put on his sock and shoe again. One hour later Art was sick and vomiting because of the nicotine that had entered his bloodstream from the snuff. The experience taught him not to judge people too quickly and never to use tobacco in any form.[229]

• After a dinner, Oscar Wilde wanted to smoke, but could not, because the women had not yet left the dining room. A lamp near him began to smoke, and his hostess told him, "Please put it out, Oscar. It's smoking." Mr. Wilde replied, "Happy lamp." By the way, a lawyer once told Mr. Wilde that Mr. Wilde's habit of giving away cigarette cases could be "expensive if indulged in indiscriminately." Mr. Wilde replied that it was "less expensive than giving jeweled garters to ladies."[230]

• In the late 19th century, Francis Hodgson Burnett, author of *A Little Princess* and *The Secret Garden*, smoked, although smoking by women was considered scandalous at the time. Often, she took a puff from a cigarette in one hand, then took a bite of a cream peppermint in her other hand.[231]

Travel

• As young men, E.B. White and his friend Howard "Cush" Cushman made a cross-country road trip in a Model T they named

"Hotspur." Among other items, they took two typewriters, as they hoped to pay for their trip by writing articles and selling them to newspapers along the way. One day, Hotspur blew out a tire, and Mr. White took one of the typewriters and walked 32 miles into a town, reciting poetry along the way. He sold the typewriter so he could buy a new tire for Hotspur.[232]

• In the late 1700s, roads in the United States were poor. Often, ruts were so bad that the drivers of stagecoaches would tell passengers to lean left or right in order to keep the stagecoach from tipping over. When the driver asked, "Now, Gentlemen, to the right," the passengers would lean to the right with half their bodies out of the stagecoach.[233]

• Charles Lindbergh didn't have a radio with him on his historic solo flight across the Atlantic Ocean in 1927 because it weighed too much. This made navigation more difficult. At one point, he flew low over a fishing vessel and shouted, "Which way to Ireland?"[234]

War

• Banksy is a British graffiti artist who is known for his satiric social commentary. In his book *Wall and Piece*, he writes, "The people who run our cities don't understand graffiti because they think nothing has the right to exist unless it makes a profit. [...] The people who truly deface our neighbourhoods are the companies that scrawl their giant slogans across buildings and buses trying to make us feel inadequate unless we buy their stuff." Banksy can be funny, as when he writes, "We can't do anything to change the world until capitalism crumbles. In the meantime we should all go shopping to console ourselves." Much consumption is mindless, but is all of it? No, of course not. In *Wall and Piece*, Banksy includes a possibly genuine extract from the diary of British soldier Colonel Mervin Willet Gonin in which Colonel Gonin writes about arriving at the Bergen-Belsen Holocaust death camp. He describes the horrors there, including piles of corpses and emaciated but living human beings. He writes, "It was shortly after the British

Red Cross arrived, though it may have no connection, that a very large quantity of lipstick arrived. This was not at all what we wanted, we were screaming for hundreds and thousands of other things and I don't know who asked for lipstick. I wish so much that I could discover who did it, it was the action of genius, sheer unadulterated brilliance. I believe nothing did more for these internees than the lipstick. Women lay in bed with no sheets and no nightie but with scarlet red lips, you saw them wandering about with nothing but a blanket over their shoulders, but with scarlet red lips. I saw a woman dead on the post-mortem table and clutched in her hand was a piece of lipstick. At last someone had done something to make them individuals again, they were someone, no longer merely the number tattooed on the arm. At last they could take an interest in their appearance. That lipstick started to give them back their humanity."[235]

• During World War II, magician Jasper Maskelyne put his talents to use in helping the British war effort in Africa. Once, he was given the task of disguising tanks so German air surveillance would not know they were present. Therefore, he designed a collapsible wooden frame that would fit over a tank. Attached to the frame were painted cloth panels that disguised the tank as a truck. On another occasion, he designed dummy submarines to float in a harbor. Several times a day, German air surveillance flew over the harbor and counted how many submarines were present. The use of the dummy submarines meant that the real submarines could depart without being missed.[236]

• During the South African War, citizens in Great Britain wondered whether the commanders sent to South Africa were competent. Tim Healy asked the Secretary of State for War, "How many horses and mules have been sent to South Africa?" After receiving the answer, Mr. Healy then asked, "And can the Right Honourable Gentleman tell me how many asses have been sent to South Africa?"[237]

• When David Niven enlisted to fight for the British in World War II, his boss, Sam Goldwyn, called him into his office, where he read him a beautiful, sentimental letter he had written. Then, with tears streaming down his face, Mr. Goldwyn buzzed a secretary, to whom he presented the letter and said, "Here's something I've written to Davey. I want you should let it leak out to the press."[238]

• During World War II, Adolf Hitler, Josef Stalin, and Winston Churchill had a meeting with God, who told them that whoever emptied the Atlantic Ocean first would win the war. Both Hitler and Stalin said that such a task was impossible, but Churchill got a bucket and filled it up, saying, "It may take a long, long time, but we are going to win this war."[239]

• During times of sacrifice, everyone must sacrifice for the war effort — well, not everyone. During World War II, gas was rationed, and most Americans could buy only four (later the number was reduced to three) gallons of gasoline a week — but members of Congress voted to allow themselves to purchase unlimited amounts of gas.[240]

Wit

• In the days of arranged marriages for Oriental women, a father and mother told their daughter that two men had offered to marry her. A rich, ugly old man in the East wanted to marry her, and a poor, handsome young man in the West wanted to marry her. The father and mother told their daughter to raise her right hand if she wanted to marry the rich, ugly old man in the East or to raise her left hand if she wanted to marry the poor, handsome young man in the West. To their surprise, their daughter raised both arms, then explained that she wanted to dine at the dinner table of the rich, ugly old man in the East, but she wanted to sleep in the bed of the poor, handsome young man in the West.[241]

• British humorist Israel Zangwill was very capable of wit. An anti-Semite once talked at excessive length during a dinner party about the desirability of the women of the island of Tahiti. Finally, Mr. Zangwill asked him whether he had noticed anything else of interest on the island. The anti-Semite looked down his nose at Mr. Zangwill and replied, "What struck me most of all is that there were no Hebrews and no pigs," "Is that so?" Mr. Zangwill said, "If you and I go there together, we shall make our fortunes." By the way, Scottish writer Andrew Lang once wrote Mr. Zangwill a letter asking him to take part in a benefit. Mr. Zangwill wrote back, "If. A. Lang will, I. Zangwill."[242]

• Dr. Samuel Johnson wrote in his famous dictionary that H seldom if ever "begins any but the first syllable of a word." John Wilkes made fun of this statement in his *Publick Advertiser*: "The author of this remark must be a man of quick appre-hension and compre-hensive genius; but I can never forgive his un-handsome be-haviour to the poor knight-hood, priest-hood, and widow-hood, nor his in-humanity to all man-hood."[243]

• Not everyone liked Oscar Wilde. At the first night of one of Mr. Wilde's plays, an enemy presented him with a rotten cabbage. Mr. Wilde replied, "A million thank-yous, my dear fellow. Every time I smell it, I shall be reminded of you."[244]

Work

• Someone asked the maggid of Zlotchov why Jews are bound to ask when their work will approach the work of their fathers: Abraham, Isaac, and Jacob. After all, isn't such a thing impossible? The maggid replied, "Just as our fathers founded new ways of serving, each a new service according to his character: one the service of love, the other that of stern justice, the third that of beauty, so each one of us in his own way shall devise something new in the light of teachings and of service, and do what has not yet been done." And when someone expressed surprise that the customs of the Seer of Lublin were different from the customs of the previous religious leader, the Seer replied, "What sort of God would be that who has only one way in which He can be served?"[245]

• Art Linkletter's father, John, was an impoverished preacher, so Art often used to do odd jobs to pick up some extra money. He once spent all day clearing rocks out of a lady's garden. When he was finally finished, the lady asked him how much he wanted for his labor. Art replied that to provide service to another human being was a reward in itself. The woman said, "How nice to know someone concerned with spiritual rather than material things. Thank you very much, little boy." Then she shut the door in his face. (Mr. Linkletter writes in his autobiography, *I Didn't Do It Alone*, that because of that incident, some of the people he did business with later in life paid a little extra for his services.)[246]

• In the 19th century, Wilbur Storey, owner of the Chicago *Times*, hired Franc B. Wilkie as his first assistant. For the first year, the two men spoke together only professionally: no personal news or greetings were ever exchanged. After a year had passed, Mr. Wilkie returned from an out-of-town assignment, and Mr. Storey asked him, "How was your trip?" Mr. Wilkie was shocked by the question, but after a moment, he answered, "I ruined a suit of clothes." Mr. Storey reached into his pocket and gave Mr. Wilkie $50.[247]

• Pope John XXIII (1881-1963) had a sense of humor. During World War I, before he became pope, he was Father Roncalli and served under Father Pignatello, chaplain general of the Italian army. Many years later, after he had become Pope, he recognized Father Pignatello during an audience and saluted him, saying, "Sergeant Roncalli, at your orders, General." By the way, Pope John XXIII was once asked how many people worked at the Vatican. He replied, "No more than half of them."[248]

• Sylvester "Pat" Weaver was such a busy radio broadcaster that he often came in to work on his day off, but he was frequently embarrassed when his boss would see him going to work at 10 a.m. because he was worried that his boss would think that he was arriving at work late.

Finally, he solved his problem by putting a sign in his car's rear window: "GOING TO WORK ON DAY OFF."[249]

• A lazy, rich man asked Dr. John Abernethy what was the best treatment for gout — a disease that afflicted the leisure class. Dr. Abernethy replied that the best treatment for gout was to live on a working wage — and to work for it.[250]

Conclusion: A Little Extra Wisdom

• After God created the first human being, he took him through the Creation, showing him all the good things there. And God told the first human being, "See my works, how fine and excellent they are! ... Do not corrupt and desolate my world; for if you corrupt it, there is no one to set it right after you."[251]

Appendix A: Book Bibliography

Adler, Bill. *Jewish Wit and Wisdom*. New York: Dell Publishing Co., Inc, 1969.

Alley, Ken. *Awkward Christian Soldiers*. Wheaton, IL: Harold Shaw Publishers, 1998.

Anecdotes of the Hour By Famous Men. New York: Hearst's International Library Company, 1914.

Banksy. *Wall and Piece*. London: Century, 2005.

Bernard, André. *Now All We Need is a Title: Famous Book Titles and How They Got That Way*. New York: W.W. Norton & Company, 1995.

Besserman, Perle and Manfred Steger. *Crazy Clouds: Zen Radicals, Rebels, and Reformers*. Boston, MA: Shambala, 1991.

Bing, Sir Rudolf. *5000 Nights at the Opera*. Garden City, NY: Doubleday and Company, Inc., 1972.

Blackman, Sushila, compiler and editor. *Graceful Exits: How Great Beings Die*. New York: Weatherhill, Inc., 1997.

Brandreth, Gyles. *Great Theatrical Disasters*. New York: St. Martin's Press, 1982.

Bryce, Ivar. *You Only Live Once: Memories of Ian Fleming*. London: Weidenfeld and Nicolson, 1984.

Buber, Martin. *The Way of Man: According to the Teaching of Hasidism*. New York: The Citadel Press, 1966.

Cantor, Eddie. *As I Remember Them*. New York: Duell, Sloan and Pearce, 1963. (Mr. Cantor's collaborator for most of these pieces was Vivian M. Bowes, to whom he gives credit on the acknowledgements page.)

Carpenter, Angelica Shirley, and Jean Shirley. *Frances Hodgson Burnett: Beyond the Secret Garden*. Minneapolis, MN: Lerner Publications Company, 1990.

Carpenter, Angelica Shirley, and Jean Shirley. *L. Frank Baum: Royal Historian of Oz*. Minneapolis, MN: Lerner Publications Company, 1992.

Chan, Luke. *101 Lessons of Tao*. Cincinnati, OH: Benefactor Books, 1995.

Charles, Helen White, collector and editor. *Quaker Chuckles and Other True Stories About Friends*. Oxford, OH: H.W. Charles, 1961.

Cleary, Thomas, translator. *Zen Antics: A Hundred Stories of Enlightenment*. Boston, MA: Shambhala Publications, Inc., 1993.

Clemens, Cyril. *Chesterton As Seen by His Contemporaries*. New York: Haskell House Publishers, Ltd., 1969.

Clemens, Cyril, editor. *Mark Twain Anecdotes*. Webster Groves, MO: Mark Twain Society, 1929.

Deedy, John. *A Book of Catholic Anecdotes*. Allen, TX: Thomas More, 1997.

Drennan, Robert E., editor. *The Algonquin Wits*. New York: The Citadel Press, 1968.

Epstein, Lawrence J. *A Treasury of Jewish Anecdotes*. Northvale, NJ: Jason Aronson, Inc., 1989.

Fadiman, James and Robert Frager. *Essential Sufism*. San Francisco, CA: HarperSanFrancisco, 1997.

Farzan, Massud. *Another Way of Laughter: A Collection of Sufi Humor*. New York: E.P. Dutton & Co., Inc., 1973.

Fesquet, Henri, collector. *Wit and Wisdom of Good Pope John*. Translated by Salvator Attanasio. New York: P.J. Kenedy & Sons, 1964.

Gaster, Moses. *The Exempla of the Rabbis: Being a Collection of Exempla, Apologues and Tales Culled from Hebrew Manuscripts and Rare Hebrew Books*. New York: Ktav Publishing House, Inc., 1968.

Glatzer, Nahum N., editor. *Hammer on the Rock: A Short Midrash Reader*. Translated by Jacob Sloan. New York: Schocken Books, 1962.

Goodman, Philip. *Rejoice in Thy Festival*. New York: Bloch Publishing Company, 1956.

Himelstein, Shmuel. *A Touch of Wisdom, A Touch of Wit*. Brooklyn, NY: Mesorah Publications, Limited, 1991.

Himelstein, Shmuel. *Words of Wisdom, Words of Wit*. Brooklyn, NY: Mesorah Publications, Ltd., 1993.

Holloway, Gary. *Saints, Demons, and Asses: Southern Preacher Anecdotes*. Bloomington, IN: Indiana University Press, 1989.

Jacobs, J. Vernon, compiler. *450 True Stories from Church History*. Grand Rapids, MI: Wm. B. Eerdmans Publishing Company, 1955.

Josephson, Judith Pinkerton. *Mother Jones: Fierce Fighter for Workers' Rights*. Minneapolis, MN: Lerner Publications Company, 1997.

Source: Kane, Jim, and Carmen Germaine Warner, editors. *Touched by a Nurse: Special Moments That Transform Lives*. Philadelphia, PA: Lippincott, 1999.

Kanner, Bernice. *The 100 Best TV Commercials ... and Why They Worked*. New York: Times Books, 1999.

Klinger, Kurt, collector. *A Pope Laughs: Stories of John XXIII*. Translated by Sally McDevitt Cunneen. New York: Holt, Rinehart and Winston, 1964.

Kramer, Barbara. *Amy Tan: Author of* The Joy Luck Club. Springfield, NJ: Enslow Publications, Inc., 1996.

Leonard, Sheldon. *And the Show Goes On: Broadway and Hollywood Adventures*. New York: Limelight, 1994.

Lilley, Stephen R. *Fighters Against American Slavery*. San Diego, CA: Lucent Books, 1999.

Monem, Nadine, editor. *Riot Grrrl: Revolution Girl Style Now!* London: Black Dog Publishing, 2007.

Linkletter, Art. *I Didn't Do It Alone: The Autobiography of Art Linkletter*. Ottawa, IL: Caroline House Publishers, Inc., 1980.

Linkletter, Art. *I Wish I'd Said That! My Favorite Ad-Libs of All Time*. Garden City, NY: Doubleday & Co., Inc., 1968.

Lisandrelli, Elaine Slivinski. *Maya Angelou: More Than a Poet*. Berkeley Heights, NJ: Enslow Publications, Inc., 1996.

Macnee, Patrick. *The Avengers and Me*. With Dave Rogers. New York: TV Books, 1997.

Marcus, Sara. *Girls to the Front: The True Story of the Riot GRRRL Revolution*. New York: Harper Perennial, 2010.

Maverick, Jr., Maury. *Texas Iconoclast*. Edited by Allan O. Kownslar. Fort Worth, TX: Texas Christian University Press, 1997

McCann, Sean, compiler. *The Wit of the Irish*. Nashville, TN: Aurora Publishers, Ltd., 1970.

McCann, Sean, compiler. *The Wit of Oscar Wilde*. New York: Barnes and Noble, Inc., 1969.

McPhaul, John J. *Deadlines and Monkeyshines: The Fabled World of Chicago Journalism*. Englewood Cliffs, NJ: Prentice-Hall, Inc. 1962.

McPhee, Nancy. *The Second Book of Insults*. Toronto, Canada: Van Nostrand Reinhold Ltd., 1981.

Mendelsohn, S. Felix. *Here's a Good One: Stories of Jewish Wit and Wisdom*. New York: Block Publishing Co., 1947.

Metil, Luana, and Jace Townsend. *The Story of Karate: From Buddhism to Bruce Lee*. Minneapolis, MN: Lerner Publications Company, 1995.

Michaels, Louis. *The Humor and Warmth of Pope John XXIII: His Anecdotes and Legends*. New York: Pocket Books, Inc., 1965.

Miller, Brandon Marie. *Just What the Doctor Ordered: The History of American Medicine*. Minneapolis, MN: Lerner Publications Company, 1997.

Mingo, Jack. *The Juicy Parts*. New York: The Berkley Publishing Group, 1996.

Morley, Robert. *Around the World in Eighty-One Years*. London: Hodder & Stoughton, 1990.

Morley, Robert. *Robert Morley's Book of Bricks*. New York: G.P. Putnam's Sons, 1979.

Mott, Robert L. *Radio Live! Television Live!: Those Golden Days When Horses Were Coconuts*. Jefferson, NC: McFarland & Company, Inc., Publishers, 2000.

Muallimoglu, Nejat. *The Wit and Wisdom of Nasraddin Hodja*. New York: Cynthia Parzych Publishing, Inc., 1986.

Nicholson, Frank Ernest. *Favorite Jokes of Famous People*. New York: E.P. Dutton & Co., Inc., 1928.

Mullen, Tom. *Laughing Out Loud and Other Religious Experiences*. Waco, TX: Word Books, 1983.

Norkin, Sam. *Drawings, Stories: Theater, Opera, Ballet, Movies*. Portsmouth, NH: Heinemann, 1994.

Old, Wendie. *Marian Wright Edelman: Fighting for Children's Rights*. Springfield, NJ: Enslow Publications, Inc., 1995.

Pearson, Hesketh. *Lives of the Wits*. New York: Harper & Row, Publishers, 1962.

Poley, Irvin C., and Ruth Verlenden Poley. *Friendly Anecdotes*. New York: Harper & Brothers, Publishers, 1950.

Porter, Alyene. *Papa was a Preacher*. New York: Abingdon Press, 1944.

Primack, Ben, adapter and editor. *The Ben Hecht Show: Impolitic Observations from the Freest Thinker of 1950s Television*. Jefferson, NC: McFarland & Company, Inc., Publishers, 1993.

Rabinowicz, Rabbi Dr. H. *A Guide to Hassidism*. New York: Thomas Yoseloff, 1960.

Richards, Dick, compiler. *The Wit of Peter Ustinov*. London: Leslie Frewin Publishers, Limited, 1969.

Rogers, Stephen, editor. *My First Year in the Classroom*. Avon, MA: Adams Media, 2009.

Rosten, Leo. *People I Have Loved, Known or Admired*. New York: McGraw-Hill Book Company, 1970.

Rowell, Edward K., editor. *Humor for Preaching and Teaching*. Grand Rapids, MI: Baker Books, 1996.

Ruth, Amy. *Mother Teresa*. Minneapolis, MN: Lerner Publications Company, 1999.

Rutkowska, Wanda. *Famous People in Anecdotes*. Warszawa: Wydawnictwa Szkolne i Pedagogiczne, 1977.

Salzberg, Sharon. *A Heart as Wide as the World: Stories on the Path to Lovingkindness*. Boston, MA: Shambhala Publications, Inc., 1997.

Salzberg, Sharon. *Lovingkindness: The Revolutionary Art of Happiness*. Boston, MA: Shambala Publications, Inc., 1995.

Samra, Cal and Rose, editors. *Holy Humor*. Colorado Springs, CO: WaterBrook Press, 1997.

Samra, Cal and Rose, editors. *More Holy Hilarity*. Colorado Springs, CO: WaterBrook Press, 1999.

Schafer, Kermit. *The Bedside Book of Celebrity Bloopers*. New York: Crown Publishers, Inc., 1984.

Schafer, Kermit. *Best of Bloopers*. New York: Avenel Books, 1973.

Schochet, Stephen. *Hollywood Stories: Short, Entertaining Anecdotes About the Stars and Legends of the Movies!* Los Angeles, CA: Hollywood Stories Publishing, 2010.

Schraff, Anne. *Coretta Scott King: Striving for Civil Rights*. Springfield, NJ: Enslow Publications, Inc., 1997.

Sessions, William H., collector. *Laughter in Quaker Grey*. York, England: William Sessions, Limited, 1966.

Sessions, William H., collector. *More Quaker Laughter*. York, England: William Sessions, Limited, 1974.

Silverman, William B. *Rabbinic Wisdom and Jewish Values*. New York: Union of American Hebrew Congregations, 1971.

Shindler, Phyllis, collector. *Raise Your Glasses*. London: Judy Piatkus, Limited, 1988.

Sigma Theta Tau International Honor Society of Nursing. *You'll Know You're a Nurse When ....* Indianapolis, IN: Sigma Theta Tau International, 2010.

Slezak, Walter. *What Time's the Next Swan?* Garden City, NY: Doubleday and Co., Inc., 1962.

Smith, H. Allen. *Buskin' With H. Allen Smith*. New York: Trident Press, 1968.

Smith, H. Allen. *The Compleat Practical Joker*. Garden City, NY: Doubleday and Company, Inc., 1953.

Sorel, Nancy Caldwell, and Edward Sorel. *First Encounters: A Book of Memorable Meetings*. New York: Alfred A. Knopf, 1994.

Spalding, Henry D. *Jewish Laffs*. Middle Village, NY: Jonathan David Publishers, Inc., 1982.

Stryk, Lucien and Takashi Ikemoto, selectors and translators. *Zen: Poems, Prayers, Sermons, Anecdotes, Interviews*. Chicago, IL: Swallow Press, 1981.

Sykes, Adam, and Iain Sproat, compilers. *The Wit of Westminster*. London: Leslie Frewin, Limited, 1967.

Taylor, Glenhall. *Before Television: The Radio Years*. New York: A.S. Barnes and Company, 1979.

Tingum, Janice. *E.B. White: The Elements of a Writer*. Minneapolis, MN: Lerner Publications Company, 1995.

Tobias, Andrew. *The Best Little Boy in the World Grows Up*. New York: Random House, 1998.

Tully, Jim. *A Dozen and One*. Hollywood, CA: Murray & Gee, Inc., Publishers, 1943.

Van Dyke, Dick. *Those Funny Kids!* Garden City, NY: Doubleday and Company, Inc., 1975.

Voskressenski, Alexei D., compiler and editor. *Cranks, Knaves, and Jokers of the Celestial*. Translated from the Chinese by Alexei Voskressenski and Vladimir Larin. Commack, NY: Nova Science Publishers, Inc., 1997.

Wadsworth, Ginger. *Laura Ingalls Wilder: Storyteller of the Prairie*. Minneapolis, MN: Lerner Publications Company, 1997.

Warren, Roz, editor. *Dyke Strippers: Lesbian Cartoonists A to Z*. Pittsburgh, PA: Cleis Press, Inc., 1995.

Wasserman, Harriet. *Handsome Is: Adventures with Saul Bellow*. New York: Fromm International Publishing Company, 1997.

Waters, John. *Shock Value*. New York: Dell Publishing Company, Inc., 1981.

Watson, Richard. *The Philosopher's Diet: How to Lose Weight and Change the World*. Boston, MA: The Atlantic Monthly Press, 1985.

Weintraub, Joseph, editor. *The Wit and Wisdom of Mae West*. New York: G.P. Putnam's Sons, 1967.

Weissman, Ginny, and Coyne Steven Sanders. *The Dick Van Dyke Show*. New York: St. Martin's Press, 1993.

White, Betty. *Here We Go Again: My Life in Television*. New York: St. Martin's Press, 1995.

Whitman, Sylvia. *Get Up and Go! The History of American Road Travel*. Minneapolis, MN: Lerner Publications Company, 1996.

Whitman, Sylvia. *V is for Victory*. Minneapolis, MN: Lerner Publications Company, 1992.

Wilkinson, Brenda. *African American Women Writers*. New York: John Wiley and Sons, Inc., 2000.

Williams, Kenneth. *Acid Drops*. London: J. M. Dent & Sons, Ltd., 1980.

Woog, Adam. *Magicians and Illusionists*. San Diego, CA: Lucent Books, 2000.

Ybarra, T.R. *Caruso: The Man of Naples and the Voice of God*. New York: Harcourt, Brace and Company, 1953.

Yearwood, Trisha. *Home Cooking with Trisha Yearwood*. With Gwen Yearwood and Beth Yearwood Bernard. New York: Clarkson Potter/Publishers, 2010.

Zall, Paul M. *The Wit and Wisdom of the Founding Fathers*. Hopewell, NJ: The Ecco Press, 1996.

Zolotow, Maurice. *No People Like Show People*. New York: Random House, 1951.

Appendix B: About the Author

It was a dark and stormy night. Suddenly a cry rang out, and on a hot summer night in 1954, Josephine, wife of Carl Bruce, gave birth to a boy — me. Unfortunately, this young married couple allowed Reuben Saturday, Josephine's brother, to name their first-born. Reuben, aka "The Joker," decided that Bruce was a nice name, so he decided to name me Bruce Bruce. I have gone by my middle name — David — ever since.

Being named Bruce David Bruce hasn't been all bad. Bank tellers remember me very quickly, so I don't often have to show an ID. It can be fun in charades, also. When I was a counselor as a teenager at Camp Echoing Hills in Warsaw, Ohio, a fellow counselor gave the signs for "sounds like" and "two words," then she pointed to a bruise on her leg twice. Bruise Bruise? Oh yeah, Bruce Bruce is the answer!

Uncle Reuben, by the way, gave me a haircut when I was in kindergarten. He cut my hair short and shaved a small bald spot on the back of my head. My mother wouldn't let me go to school until the bald spot grew out again.

Of all my brothers and sisters (six in all), I am the only transplant to Athens, Ohio. I was born in Newark, Ohio, and have lived all around Southeastern Ohio. However, I moved to Athens to go to Ohio University and have never left.

At Ohio U, I never could make up my mind whether to major in English or Philosophy, so I got a bachelor's degree with a double major in both areas, then I added a Master of Arts degree in English and a Master of Arts degree in Philosophy. Yes, I have my MAMA degree.

Currently, and for a long time to come (I eat fruits and veggies), I am spending my retirement writing books such as *Nadia Comaneci: Perfect 10*, *The Funniest People in Comedy*, *Homer's* Iliad: *A Retelling in Prose*, and *William Shakespeare's* Hamlet: *A Retelling in Prose*.

If all goes well, I will publish one or two books a year for the rest of my life. (On the other hand, a good way to make God laugh is to tell Her your plans.)

By the way, my sister Brenda Kennedy writes romances such as *A New Beginning* and *Shattered Dreams*.

Appendix C: Some Books by David Bruce

Anecdote Collections

250 Anecdotes About Religion
250 Anecdotes About Religion: Volume 2
The Coolest People in Art: 250 Anecdotes
The Coolest People in Books: 250 Anecdotes
The Coolest People in Comedy: 250 Anecdotes
Don't Fear the Reaper: 250 Anecdotes
The Funniest People in Art: 250 Anecdotes
The Funniest People in Books: 250 Anecdotes
The Funniest People in Books, Volume 2: 250 Anecdotes
The Funniest People in Books, Volume 3: 250 Anecdotes
The Funniest People in Comedy: 250 Anecdotes
The Funniest People in Dance: 250 Anecdotes
The Funniest People in Families: 250 Anecdotes
The Funniest People in Families, Volume 2: 250 Anecdotes
The Funniest People in Families, Volume 3: 250 Anecdotes
The Funniest People in Families, Volume 4: 250 Anecdotes
The Funniest People in Families, Volume 5: 250 Anecdotes
The Funniest People in Families, Volume 6: 250 Anecdotes
The Funniest People in Movies: 250 Anecdotes
The Funniest People in Music: 250 Anecdotes
The Funniest People in Music, Volume 2: 250 Anecdotes
The Funniest People in Music, Volume 3: 250 Anecdotes
The Funniest People in Neighborhoods: 250 Anecdotes
The Funniest People in Relationships: 250 Anecdotes
The Funniest People in Sports: 250 Anecdotes
The Funniest People in Sports, Volume 2: 250 Anecdotes
The Funniest People in Television and Radio: 250 Anecdotes
The Funniest People in Theater: 250 Anecdotes
The Funniest People Who Live Life: 250 Anecdotes
The Funniest People Who Live Life, Volume 2: 250 Anecdotes
The Kindest People Who Do Good Deeds, Volume 1: 250 Anecdotes
The Kindest People Who Do Good Deeds, Volume 2: 250 Anecdotes
Maximum Cool: 250 Anecdotes

The Most Interesting People in Movies: 250 Anecdotes

The Most Interesting People in Politics and History: 250 Anecdotes

The Most Interesting People in Politics and History, Volume 2: 250 Anecdotes

The Most Interesting People in Politics and History, Volume 3: 250 Anecdotes

The Most Interesting People in Religion: 250 Anecdotes

The Most Interesting People in Sports: 250 Anecdotes

The Most Interesting People Who Live Life: 250 Anecdotes

The Most Interesting People Who Live Life, Volume 2: 250 Anecdotes

Resist Psychic Death: 250 Anecdotes

Retellings of a Classic Work of Literature

Ben Jonson's The Alchemist: *A Retelling*

Ben Jonson's The Arraignment, or Poetaster: *A Retelling*

Ben Jonson's Bartholomew Fair: *A Retelling*

Ben Jonson's The Case is Altered: *A Retelling*

Ben Jonson's Catiline's Conspiracy: *A Retelling*

Ben Jonson's The Devil is an Ass: *A Retelling*

Ben Jonson's Epicene: *A Retelling*

Ben Jonson's Every Man in His Humor: *A Retelling*

Ben Jonson's Every Man Out of His Humor: *A Retelling*

Ben Jonson's The Fountain of Self-Love, or Cynthia's Revels: *A Retelling*

Ben Jonson's The Magnetic Lady, or Humors Reconciled: *A Retelling*

Ben Jonson's The New Inn, or The Light Heart: *A Retelling*

Ben Jonson's Sejanus' Fall: *A Retelling*

Ben Jonson's The Staple of News: *A Retelling*

Ben Jonson's A Tale of a Tub: *A Retelling*

Ben Jonson's Volpone, or the Fox: *A Retelling*

Christopher Marlowe's Complete Plays: Retellings

Christopher Marlowe's Dido, Queen of Carthage: *A Retelling*

Christopher Marlowe's Doctor Faustus: *Retellings of the 1604 A-Text and of the 1616 B-Text*

Christopher Marlowe's Edward II: *A Retelling*

Christopher Marlowe's The Massacre at Paris: *A Retelling*

Christopher Marlowe's The Rich Jew of Malta: *A Retelling*

Christopher Marlowe's Tamburlaine, Parts 1 and 2: *Retellings*

Dante's Divine Comedy: A Retelling in Prose

Dante's Inferno: *A Retelling in Prose*

Dante's Purgatory: *A Retelling in Prose*

Dante's Paradise: *A Retelling in Prose*

The Famous Victories of Henry V: *A Retelling*

From the Iliad *to the* Odyssey*: A Retelling in Prose of Quintus of Smyrna's* Posthomerica

George Chapman, Ben Jonson, and John Marston's Eastward Ho! *A Retelling*

George Peele's The Arraignment of Paris: *A Retelling*

George Peele's The Battle of Alcazar: *A Retelling*

George's Peele's David and Bathsheba, and the Tragedy of Absalom: *A Retelling*

George Peele's Edward I: *A Retelling*

George Peele's The Old Wives' Tale: *A Retelling*

George-a-Greene: *A Retelling*

The History of King Leir: *A Retelling*

Homer's Iliad: *A Retelling in Prose*

Homer's Odyssey: *A Retelling in Prose*

J.W. Gent.'s The Valiant Scot: *A Retelling*

Jason and the Argonauts: A Retelling in Prose of Apollonius of Rhodes' Argonautica

John Ford: Eight Plays Translated into Modern English

John Ford's The Broken Heart: *A Retelling*

John Ford's The Fancies, Chaste and Noble: *A Retelling*

John Ford's The Lady's Trial: *A Retelling*

John Ford's The Lover's Melancholy: *A Retelling*

John Ford's Love's Sacrifice: *A Retelling*

John Ford's Perkin Warbeck: *A Retelling*

John Ford's The Queen: *A Retelling*

John Ford's 'Tis Pity She's a Whore: *A Retelling*

John Lyly's Campaspe: *A Retelling*

John Lyly's Endymion, The Man in the Moon: *A Retelling*

John Lyly's Galatea: *A Retelling*

John Lyly's Love's Metamorphosis: *A Retelling*

John Lyly's Midas: *A Retelling*

John Lyly's Mother Bombie: *A Retelling*

John Lyly's Sappho and Phao: *A Retelling*

John Lyly's The Woman in the Moon: *A Retelling*

John Webster's The White Devil: *A Retelling*

King Edward III: *A Retelling*

Mankind: *A Medieval Morality Play* (A Retelling)

Margaret Cavendish's The Unnatural Tragedy: *A Retelling*

The Merry Devil of Edmonton: *A Retelling*

Robert Greene's Friar Bacon and Friar Bungay: *A Retelling*

The Taming of a Shrew: *A Retelling*

Tarlton's Jests: A Retelling

Thomas Middleton's A Chaste Maid in Cheapside: *A Retelling*

Thomas Middleton's Women Beware Women: *A Retelling*

Thomas Middleton and William Rowley's The Changeling: *A Retelling*

The Trojan War and Its Aftermath: Four Ancient Epic Poems

Virgil's Aeneid: *A Retelling in Prose*

William Shakespeare's 1 Henry IV, aka Henry IV, Part 1: *A Retelling in Prose*

William Shakespeare's 2 Henry IV, aka Henry IV, Part 2: *A Retelling in Prose*

William Shakespeare's Antony and Cleopatra: *A Retelling in Prose*

William Shakespeare's As You Like It: *A Retelling in Prose*

William Shakespeare's The Comedy of Errors: *A Retelling in Prose*

William Shakespeare's Cymbeline: *A Retelling in Prose William*

Shakespeare's Hamlet: *A Retelling in Prose*

William Shakespeare's Henry V: *A Retelling in Prose*

William Shakespeare's Julius Caesar: *A Retelling in Prose*

William Shakespeare's King Lear: *A Retelling in Prose*

William Shakespeare's Macbeth: *A Retelling in Prose*

William Shakespeare's Measure for Measure: *A Retelling in Prose*

William Shakespeare's The Merchant of Venice: *A Retelling in Prose*

William Shakespeare's The Merry Wives of Windsor: *A Retelling in Prose*

William Shakespeare's A Midsummer Night's Dream: *A Retelling in Prose*

William Shakespeare's Much Ado About Nothing: *A Retelling in Prose*

William Shakespeare's Othello: *A Retelling in Prose*

William Shakespeare's Pericles, Prince of Tyre: *A Retelling in Prose*

William Shakespeare's Richard III: *A Retelling in Prose*

William Shakespeare's Romeo and Juliet: *A Retelling in Prose*

William Shakespeare's The Taming of the Shrew: *A Retelling in Prose*

William Shakespeare's The Tempest: *A Retelling in Prose*

William Shakespeare's Titus Andronicus: *A Retelling in Prose*

William Shakespeare's Twelfth Night: *A Retelling in Prose*

William Shakespeare's The Two Gentlemen of Verona: *A Retelling in Prose*

William Shakespeare's The Winter's Tale: *A Retelling in Prose*

[1] Source: Jim Kane and Carmen Germaine Warner, editors, *Touched by a Nurse: Special Moments That Transform Lives*, p. 80.

[2] Source: Maury Maverick, Jr., *Texas Iconoclast*, p. 16.

[3] Source: Luke O'Neil, "Gym Rat Control." *Slate*. 9 May 2011 <http://www.slate.com/id/2293368/>.

[4] Source: Stephen R. Lilley, *Fighters Against American Slavery*, p. 19.

[5] Source: Judith Pinkerton Josephson, *Mother Jones: Fierce Fighter for Workers' Rights*, pp. 63- 68.

[6] Source: Maurice Zolotow, *No People Like Show People*, p. 8.

[7] Source: Gyles Brandreth, *Great Theatrical Disasters*, p. 55.

[8] Source: Ginny Weissman and Coyne Steven Sanders, *The Dick Van Dyke Show*, p. 6.

[9] Source: Gyles Brandreth, *Great Theatrical Disasters*, p. 89.

[10] Source: Sam Norkin, *Drawings, Stories*, p. 98.

[11] Source: Bernice Kanner, *The 100 Best TV Commercials*, p. 174.

[12] Source: Helen White Charles, collector and editor, *Quaker Chuckles*, p. 117.

[13] Source: Ivar Bryce, *You Only Live Once*, pp. 31-32.

[14] Source: Sam Norkin, *Drawings, Stories*, p. 221.

[15] Source: Eddie Cantor, *As I Remember Them*, p. 56.

[16] Source: Louis Michaels, *The Humor and Warmth of Pope John XXIII*, p. 57.

[17] Source: Perle Besserman and Manfred Steger, *Crazy Clouds*, p. 53.

[18] Source: Betty White, *Here We Go Again*, p. 84.

[19] Source: Barbara Kramer, *Amy Tan: Author of* The Joy Luck Club, pp. 63, 73.

[20] Source: Ivar Bryce, *You Only Live Once*, p. 83.

[21] Source: Cyril Clemens, *Chesterton As Seen by His Contemporaries*, p. 151.

[22] Source: Sir Rudolf Bing, *5000 Nights at the Opera*, p. 91.

[23] Source: Phyllis Shindler, collector, *Raise Your Glasses*, pp. 85-86.

[24] Source: Harriet Wasserman, *Handsome Is: Adventures with Saul Bellow*, p. 127.

[25] Source: H. Allen Smith, *Buskin' With H. Allen Smith*, p. 85.

[26]Source: Cyril Clemens, *Chesterton As Seen by His Contemporaries*, pp. 16-17, 137-138.

[27]Source: André Bernard, *Now All We Need is a Title*, pp. 99-100.

[28]Source: Angelica Shirley Carpenter and Jean Shirley, *L. Frank Baum: Royal Historian of Oz*, p. 10.

[29] Source: Jim Kane and Carmen Germaine Warner, editors, *Touched by a Nurse: Special Moments That Transform Lives*, p. 101.

[30] Source: Wuapinmon, post on "The 'Kids Say the Darndest Things' thread." <Cougaruteforum.com. http://cougaruteforum.com/showthread.php?t=16907>. Accessed on 16 April 2011. Also: a post by "The Fourth Nephite."

[31]Source: Dick Richards, compiler, *The Wit of Peter Ustinov*, pp. 51, 79.

[32]Source: Cal and Rose Samra, *Holy Humor*, p. 201.

[33]Source: Alyene Porter, *Papa was a Preacher*, p. 21.

[34]Source: Kermit Schafer, *The Bedside Book of Celebrity Bloopers*, pp. 2-3.

[35]Source: Wanda Rutkowska, *Famous People in Anecdotes*, pp. 40-41.

[36]Source: Ken Alley, *Awkward Christian Soldiers*, p. 37.

[37]Source: William H. Sessions, collector, *Laughter in Quaker Grey*, pp. 69-70.

[38]Source: Cal and Rose Samra, *More Holy Hilarity*, pp. 149-150.

[39] Source: T.R. Ybarra, *Caruso: The Man of Naples and the Voice of God*, p. 263.

[40]Source: Sheldon Leonard, *And the Show Goes On*, p. 50.

[41]Source: Kurt Klinger, *A Pope Laughs*, p. 90.

[42]Source: William H. Sessions, collector, *Laughter in Quaker Grey*, p. 24.

[43]Source: Shmuel Himelstein, *Words of Wisdom, Words of Wit*, p. 260.

[44]Source: Paul M. Zall, *The Wit and Wisdom of the Founding Fathers*, pp. 99, 110.

[45]Source: Philip Goodman, *Rejoice in Thy Festival*, p. 218.

[46]Source: Massud Farzan, *Another Way of Laughter*, p. 87.

[47]Source: S. Felix Mendelsohn, *Here's a Good One*, pp. 175-176.

[48]Source: Kenneth Williams, *Acid Drops*, p. 90.

[49]Source: Nancy Caldwell Sorel and Edward Sorel, *First Encounters*, p. 31.

[50]Source: Sean McCann, compiler, *The Wit of the Irish*, p. 28.

[51]Source: Ben Primack, adapter and editor, *The Ben Hecht Show*, p. 185.

[52] Source: John J. McPhaul, *Deadlines and Monkeyshines: The Fabled World of Chicago Journalism*, p. 71.

[53] Source: Angelica Shirley Carpenter and Jean Shirley, *L. Frank Baum: Royal Historian of Oz*, pp. 36-37.

[54] Source: Andrew Tobias, "It's Not His Call." Andrewtobias.com. 18 May 2011 <http://www.andrewtobias.com/newcolumns/110518.html>.

[55] Source: Sean McCann, compiler, *The Wit of the Irish*, pp. 117-118, 123.

[56] Source: Robert Morley, *Robert Morley's Book of Bricks*, pp. 81-82.

[57] Source: Sushila Blackman, compiler and editor, *Graceful Exits*, p. 33.

[58] Source: Sharon Salzberg, *A Heart as Wide as the World*, pp. 34-35.

[59] Source: S. Felix Mendelsohn, *Here's a Good One*, p. 144.

[60] Source: Massud Farzan, *Another Way of Laughter*, p. 25.

[61] Source: J. Vernon Jacobs, compiler, *450 True Stories from Church History*, p. 66.

[62] Source: Nahum N. Glatzer, editor, *Hammer on the Rock*, p. 65.

[63] Source: Sushila Blackman, compiler and editor, *Graceful Exits*, p. 82.

[64] Source: Robert Morley, *Around the World in Eighty-One Years*, p. 24.

[65] Source: Kari-Lynn Winters, "Rumors," which is collected in this book: *My First Year in the Classroom*, edited by Stephen Rogers.

[66] Source: William B. Silverman, *Rabbinic Wisdom and Jewish Values*, pp. 208-209.

[67] Source: Brandon Marie Miller, *Just What the Doctor Ordered: The History of American Medicine*, pp. 62-63, 68.

[68] Source: Moses Gaster, *The Exempla of the Rabbis*, p. 171.

[69] Source: John Deedy, *A Book of Catholic Anecdotes*, p. 48.

[70] Source: Brandon Marie Miller, *Just What the Doctor Ordered: The History of American Medicine*, pp. 52-53.

[71] Source: Elaine Slivinski Lisandrelli, *Maya Angelou: More Than a Poet*, pp. 32-33.

[72] Source: Lucien Stryk and Takashi Ikemoto, selectors and translators, *Zen: Poems, Prayers, Sermons, Anecdotes, Interviews*, pp. xxxii and 131.

[73] Source: William H. Sessions, collector, *More Quaker Laughter*, p. 106.

[74]Source: Rabbi Dr. H. Rabinowicz, *A Guide to Hassidism*, p. 94.

[75]Source: Wendie Old, *Marian Wright Edelman: Fighting for Children's Rights*, p. 29.

[76]Source: Dick Van Dyke, *Those Funny Kids!*, p. 123.

[77]Source: Henry D. Spalding, *Jewish Laffs*, p. 41.

[78]Source: Shmuel Himelstein, *A Touch of Wisdom, A Touch of Wit*, p. 22.

[79]Source: Martin Buber, *The Way of Man*, p. 15.

[80]Source: Elaine Slivinski Lisandrelli, *Maya Angelou: More Than a Poet*, pp. 61-62.

[81]Source: Perle Besserman and Manfred Steger, *Crazy Clouds*, p. 67.

[82] Source: John C. Ensslin, "A calling to educate children." *Rocky Mountain News* (Denver, CO). 21 June 2005 <http://www.goodnewsblog.com/2005/06/21/a-calling-to-educate-children>.

[83]Source: Richard Watson, *The Philosopher's Diet*, p. 85.

[84]Source: Sharon Salzberg, *A Heart as Wide as the World*, pp. 32-33.

[85]Source: Moses Gaster, *The Exempla of the Rabbis*, pp. 99-100.

[86]Source: Thomas Cleary, translator, *Zen Antics*, p. 55.

[87]Source: Jack Mingo, *The Juicy Parts*, pp. 66-67.

[88] Source: Sanford Pinsker, "You Can't Go Home Again, with Apologies to Thomas Wolfe." *The Irascible Professor*. 20 April 2011 <http://irascibleprofessor.com/comments-04-20-11.htm>.

[89] Source: Homa Khaleeli, "Amazing photograph of the space shuttle Endeavour." *The Guardian*. 17 May 2011 <http://www.guardian.co.uk/science/2011/may/17/photograph-space-shuttle-endeavour-aeroplane#>. Also: Jon Norris, "Woman gets boned by media, Twitpic to blame." Unplugged.rcrwireless.com. 18 May 2011 <http://unplugged.rcrwireless.com/index.php/20110518/news/9014/woman-gets-boned-by-media-twitpic-to-blame/>. Also: Matt Sedensky, "Woman's plane photos of space shuttle go viral." Associated Press. 17 May 2011 <http://hosted.ap.org/dynamic/stories/U/US_SPACE_SHUTTLE_PHOTOS?SITE=AP&SECTION=HOME&TEMPLATE=DE

[90] Source: Karen Zarker, "20 Questions: Simon Van Booy." PopMatters. 5 July 2011 <http://www.popmatters.com/pm/feature/144448-20-questions-simon-van-booy/>.

[91] Source: Trisha Yearwood, *Home Cooking with Trisha Yearwood*, pp. 93, 155.

[92] Source: Shmuel Himelstein, *Words of Wisdom, Words of Wit*, pp. 31-32.

[93] Source: Cal and Rose Samra, *More Holy Hilarity*, p. 16.

[94] Source: William B. Silverman, *Rabbinic Wisdom and Jewish Values*, p. 207.

[95] Source: John Deedy, *A Book of Catholic Anecdotes*, p. 56.

[96] Source: Richard Watson, *The Philosopher's Diet*, p. 97.

[97] Source: Robert Morley, *Robert Morley's Book of Bricks*, p. 13.

[98] Source: Sean McCann, compiler, *The Wit of Oscar Wilde*, pp. 9-10.

[99] Source: Robert E. Drennan, ed., *The Algonquin Wits*, p. 13.

[100] Source: Patrick Macnee, *The Avengers and Me*, p. 119.

[101] Source: William H. Sessions, collector, *More Quaker Laughter*, p. 88.

[102] Source: Roz Warren, editor, *Dyke Strippers: Lesbian Cartoonists A to Z*, pp. 23, 132, 189.

[103] Source: Andrew Tobias, *The Best Little Boy in the World Grows Up*, pp. 88, 221.

[104] Source: John Waters, *Shock Value*, p. 149.

[105] Source: Jodi R. Scott, "A Random Act of Kindness." People and Possibilities. http://www.peopleandpossibilities.com/33kindnessstories2.html. Accessed on 12 May 2011.

[106] Source: Alexei D. Voskressenski, compiler and editor, *Cranks, Knaves, and Jokers of the Celestial*, p. 16.

[107] Source: Craig Wall, "Homeless Chicago Man Donates Thousands to Down-On-Her-Luck Banker." FOX Chicago News. 12 May 2011 <http://www.myfoxchicago.com/dpp/news/metro/homeless-chicago-man-curtis-jackson-donates-thousands-to-sandy-lost-job-son-truck-hotel-20110511>.

[108] Source: "Honest taxi driver returns $50,000 in dollar bills to businessman after finding it on back seat of his Cambridge cab (and pockets a $500 tip)." *Daily*

Mail. 25 April 2011 <http://www.dailymail.co.uk/news/article-1380147/Cab-believe-Honest-cabbie-returns-50-000-businessman-left-taxi.html>.

[109] Source: "Parrot leads couple to quit smoking." Reuters. 5 August 2004 <http://www.telegraphindia.com/1040806/asp/foreign/story_3590429.asp>.

[110] Source: Sergio Robin, "Pocketbook Found on East Side of Manhattan – Honesty Story #23." Honesty Blog. 28 November 2007 <http://honestyblog.com/2007/11/28/pocket-book-found-on-east-side-of-manhattan-honesty-story-23/>.

[111] Source: "Honest cabbie returns diamonds (Afghan immigrant does the right thing)." News 24 (South Africa). 17 November 2005 <http://www.freerepublic.com/focus/f-news/1524541/posts>.

[112] Source: Tony, "Returned Wallet at Walmart – Honesty Story #21." Honesty Blog. 13 July 2007 <http://honestyblog.com/2007/07/13/returned-wallet-at-walmart-honesty-story-21/>.

[113]Source: Shmuel Himelstein, *A Touch of Wisdom, A Touch of Wit*, p. 196.

[114] Source: SadieMadison, "A Little Kindness Comes Back a Dinner." Helpothers.org. 26 February 2011 <http://www.helpothers.org/story.php?sid=24942>.

[115] Source: Stephen Schochet, *Hollywood Stories*, pp. 253-254.

[116] Source: Ritac, "A Random Act of Kindness Story." People and Possibilities. <http://www.peopleandpossibilities.com/33kindnessstories2.html>. Accessed on 10 May 2011.

[117] Source: T.R. Ybarra, *Caruso: The Man of Naples and the Voice of God*, pp. 212-213.

[118] Source: Anwahs, "Halloween Candy Robbery." Daily good.org. 22 March 2008 <http://www.dailygood.org/view.php?qid=4259>.

[119] Source: Ian Ith, "Mountaineer, 77, saved lives of six climbers on K2 in '53." *Seattle Times.* 24 September 2004 <http://seattletimes.nwsource.com/html/localnews/2002045151_schoeningobit24m.html>. Also: "Pete Schoening." Wikipedia. <http://en.wikipedia.org/wiki/Pete_Schoening>. Accessed 18 June 2011.

[120] Source: "12 yo rescued from sea." Good News Blog. 21 September 2005 <http://www.goodnewsblog.com/2005/09/21/12-yo-rescued-from-sea>.

[121] Source: Elva Ramirez, "Plunge Girl's Day Care Hit For Violations." *New York Daily News*. 12 August 2005 <http://articles.nydailynews.com/2005-08-12/news/18315512_1_health-department-rooftop-playground>. Also: "Miracle catch saves girl." Good News Blog, 11 August 2005 <http://www.goodnewsblog.com/2005/08/11/miracle-catch-saves-girl>.

[122] Source: Stephen R. Lilley, *Fighters Against American Slavery*, pp. 73-75.

[123] Source: Frank Ernest Nicholson, *Favorite Jokes of Famous People*, pp. 174-175.

[124] Source: Ginger Wadsworth, *Laura Ingalls Wilder: Storyteller of the Prairie*, p. 59.

[125] Source: Adam Woog, *Magicians and Illusionists*, p. 58.

[126] Source: Ken Alley, *Awkward Christian Soldiers*, p. 24.

[127] Source: Gary Holloway, *Saints, Demons, and Asses*, pp. 35, 60-61.

[128] Source: Paul M. Zall, *The Wit and Wisdom of the Founding Fathers*, pp. 152-153.

[129] Source: Sigma Theta Tau International Honor Society of Nursing, *You'll Know You're a Nurse When ...*, p. 68.

[130] Source: Kermit Schafer, *Best of Bloopers*, p. 51.

[131] Source: Ginger Wadsworth, *Laura Ingalls Wilder: Storyteller of the Prairie*, p. 78.

[132] Source: Barbara Kramer, *Amy Tan: Author of* The Joy Luck Club, pp. 42-43.

[133] Source: Andrew Tobias, *The Best Little Boy in the World Grows Up*, p. 259.

[134] Source: Nancy McPhee, *The Second Book of Insults*, p. 97.

[135] Source: Leo Rosten, *People I Have Loved, Known or Admired*, p. 254.

[136] Source: Julia Downes, "Riot Grrrl: The Legacy and Contemporary Landscape of DIY Feminist Cultural Activism," pp. 41-42. Collected in this book: Nadine Monem, editor. *Riot Grrrl: Revolution Girl Style Now!* Also: Sara Marcus, *Girls to the Front: The True Story of the Riot GRRRL Revolution*, p. 80.

[137] Source: Robert L. Mott, *Radio Live! Television Live!*, p. 30.

[138] Source: Sheldon Leonard, *And the Show Goes On*, p. 62.

[139]Source: Robert L. Mott, *Radio Live! Television Live!*, pp. 38, 161.

[140]Source: Sylvia Whitman, *V is for Victory*, p. 41.

[141]Source: Kermit Schafer, *Best of Bloopers*, p. 97.

[142]Source: Kurt Klinger, *A Pope Laughs*, pp. 28, 51.

[143]Source: Frank Ernest Nicholson, *Favorite Jokes of Famous People*, pp. 32-33.

[144]Source: Lawrence J. Epstein, *A Treasury of Jewish Anecdotes*, p. 4.

[145]Source: Bill Adler, *Jewish Wit and Wisdom*, pp. 121-122.

[146]Source: Leo Rosten, *People I Have Loved, Known or Admired*, p. 65. Also: Source: Eddie Cantor, *As I Remember Them*, p. 104.

[147]Source: Cal and Rose Samra, *Holy Humor*, p. 218.

[148]Source: James Fadiman and Robert Frager, *Essential Sufism*, p. 188.

[149]Source: Cyril Clemens, editor, *Mark Twain Anecdotes*, p. 29.

[150]Source: John Waters, *Shock Value*, pp. 94-95.

[151]Source: Bernice Kanner, *The 100 Best TV Commercials*, pp. 153- 154.

[152]Source: Anne Schraff, *Coretta Scott King: Striving for Civil Rights*, p. 89.

[153]Source: Betty White, *Here We Go Again*, p. 65.

[154]Source: Alexei D. Voskressenski, compiler and editor, *Cranks, Knaves, and Jokers of the Celestial*, p. 34.

[155]Source: Robert Morley, *Around the World in Eighty-One Years*, p. 98.

[156]Source: Roz Warren, editor, *Dyke Strippers: Lesbian Cartoonists A to Z*, p. 42.

[157]Source: Angelica Shirley Carpenter and Jean Shirley, *Frances Hodgson Burnett: Beyond the Secret Garden*, pp. 44- 45.

[158] Source: Joseph Epstein, "Duh, Bor-ing." *Commentary Magazine*. June 2011 <http://www.commentarymagazine.com/article/duh-boring/>.

[159]Source: Brenda Wilkinson, *African American Women Writers*, p. 112.

[160]Source: Jim Tully, *A Dozen and One*, p-. 139, 141-142.

[161]Source: Judith Pinkerton Josephson, *Mother Jones: Fierce Fighter for Workers' Rights*, pp. 132-133.

[162]Source: Joseph Weintraub, editor, *The Wit and Wisdom of Mae West*, p. 32.

[163]Source: Maurice Zolotow, *No People Like Show People*, p. 292.

[164]Source: Walter Slezak, *What Time's the Next Swan?*, pp. 11-12.

[165]Source: Nancy McPhee, *The Second Book of Insults*, p. 78-79.

[166]Source: Sir Rudolf Bing, *5000 Nights at the Opera*, p. 246.

[167]Source: Kermit Schafer, *The Bedside Book of Celebrity Bloopers*, p. 10.

[168]Source: Joseph Weintraub, editor, *The Wit and Wisdom of Mae West*, p. 79.

[169]Source: Janice Tingum, *E.B. White: The Elements of a Writer*, pp. 19, 27.

[170]Source: Edward K. Rowell, editor, *Humor for Preaching and Teaching*, p. 103.

[171] Source: Austin Fenner, "Osama Jeers Didn't Stop Sikh Marathon Man, 92." *New York Daily News*. 14 November 2003 <http://articles.nydailynews.com/2003-11-14/news/18238551_1_sikh-religion-ellis-island-medal>. Also: Jose Martinez, "92-year-old Sikh set to go distance." *New York Daily News*. 2 November 2003 < http://articles.nydailynews.com/2003-11-02/news/18242501_1_sikh-culture-five-boroughs-new-york-city-marathon>.

[172]Source: Helen White Charles, collector and editor, *Quaker Chuckles*, p. 5.

[173]Source: Sir Rudolf Bing, *5000 Nights at the Opera*, p. 185.

[174]Source: Art Linkletter, *I Wish I'd Said That!*, p. 105.

[175] Source: Michael Inbar, "Born to save sister's life, she's 'glad I am in this family.'" *Today*. 2011 <http://today.msnbc.msn.com/id/43265160/ns/today-good_news/>. Accessed on 3 June 2011.

[176]Source: Harriet Wasserman, *Handsome Is: Adventures with Saul Bellow*, pp. 110-111.

[177]Source: Robert E. Drennan, ed., *The Algonquin Wits*, p. 32.

[178]Source: Anne Schraff, *Coretta Scott King: Striving for Civil Rights*, pp. 72-73.

[179]Source: Nejat Muallimoglu, *The Wit and Wisdom of Nasraddin Hodja*, p. 56.

[180]Source: Sharon Salzberg, *Lovingkindness*, pp. 140-141.

[181]Source: Maury Maverick, Jr., *Texas Iconoclast*, pp. 88-89.

[182]Source: Wendie Old, *Marian Wright Edelman: Fighting for Children's Rights*, pp. 50, 52.

[183]Source: Hesketh Pearson, *Lives of the Wits*, p. 152, 160, 162.

[184]Source: Jim Tully, *A Dozen and One*, p. 209.

[185]Source: Walter Slezak, *What Time's the Next Swan?*, pp. 77-78.

[186]Source: H. Allen Smith, *The Compleat Practical Joker*, p. 269.

[187]Source: James Fadiman and Robert Frager, *Essential Sufism*, pp. 237-38.

[188]Source: Rabbi Dr. H. Rabinowicz, *A Guide to Hassidism*, p. 103.

[189]Source: Philip Goodman, *Rejoice in Thy Festival*, p. 101.

[190] Source: Banksy, *Wall and Piece*, pp. 13, 58, 205.

[191]Source: Cyril Clemens, editor, *Mark Twain Anecdotes*, p. 13.

[192]Source: Sharon Salzberg, *Lovingkindness*, pp. 7-8.

[193]Source: Ginny Weissman and Coyne Steven Sanders, *The Dick Van Dyke Show*, p. 35.

[194] Source: *Anecdotes of the Hour By Famous Men*, pp. 28-29.

[195] Source: Luke Chan, *101 Lessons of Tao*, p. 53.

[196]Source: Luana Metil and Jace Townsend, *The Story of Karate: From Buddhism to Bruce Lee*, pp. 52, 55.

[197] Source: Patrick Kingsley, "How far would you go to get a job?" *Guardian* (UK). 17 July 2011 <http://www.guardian.co.uk/education/2011/jul/17/how-far-to-get-a-job>.

[198]Source: Bill Adler, *Jewish Wit and Wisdom*, pp. 128-129.

[199] Source: Sigma Theta Tau International Honor Society of Nursing, *You'll Know You're a Nurse When ...*, p. 79.

[200]Source: Sir Rudolf Bing, *5000 Nights at the Opera*, pp. 261-262.

[201]Source: Irvin C. Poley and Ruth Verlenden Poley, *Friendly Anecdotes*, p. 32.

[202]Source: Patrick Macnee, *The Avengers and Me*, p. 83.

[203]Source: Henry D. Spalding, *Jewish Laffs*, p. 43.

[204]Source: Lucien Stryk and Takashi Ikemoto, selectors and translators, *Zen: Poems, Prayers, Sermons, Anecdotes, Interviews*, p. 117.

[205]Source: Sylvia Whitman, *Get Up and Go! The History of American Road Travel*, p. 61.

[206]Source: Nejat Muallimoglu, *The Wit and Wisdom of Nasraddin Hodja*, p. 72.

[207]Source: Dick Van Dyke, *Those Funny Kids!*, p. 84.

[208]Source: J. Vernon Jacobs, compiler, *450 True Stories from Church History*, p. 115.

[209]Source: Lawrence J. Epstein, *A Treasury of Jewish Anecdotes*, pp. 158-159.

[210]Source: Brenda Wilkinson, *African American Women Writers*, p. 18.

[211]Source: Tom Mullen, *Laughing Out Loud and Other Religious Experiences*, p. 35.

[212]Source: Ben Primack, adapter and editor, *The Ben Hecht Show*, pp. 76-77.

[213]Source: Irvin C. Poley and Ruth Verlenden Poley, *Friendly Anecdotes*, pp. 39-40.

[214]Source: Phyllis Shindler, collector, *Raise Your Glasses*, p. 95.

[215]Source: Alyene Porter, *Papa was a Preacher*, pp. 16, 27.

[216]Source: Amy Ruth, *Mother Teresa*, pp. 69, 87.

[217]Source: Louis Michaels, *The Humor and Warmth of Pope John XXIII*, pp. 27, 38.

[218]Source: Edward K. Rowell, editor, *Humor for Preaching and Teaching*, p. 132.

[219]Source: H. Allen Smith, *Buskin' With H. Allen Smith*, pp. 194-195.

[220]Source: Amy Ruth, *Mother Teresa*, p. 91.

[221]Source: Nancy Caldwell Sorel and Edward Sorel, *First Encounters*, p. 67.

[222]Source: H. Allen Smith, *The Compleat Practical Joker*, p. 290.

[223] Source: Cecilia, "My Mother's Simple Lesson in Kindness." Helpothers.org. 8 April 2011 <http://www.helpothers.org/story.php?sid=25694>.

[224] Source: "2 brothers buy food, get lost, start charity." Good News Blog. 16 August 2005 <http://www.goodnewsblog.com/category/charity/page/20>. Also: "Rancho Feliz." <https://www.ranchofeliz.com/>. Accessed 22 July 2011.

[225] Source: Stephen Schochet, *Hollywood Stories*, p. 242.

[226]Source: Art Linkletter, *I Wish I'd Said That!*, p. 27.

[227]Source: André Bernard, *Now All We Need is a Title*, p. 118.

[228]Source: Hesketh Pearson, *Lives of the Wits*, p. 91.

[229]Source: Art Linkletter, *I Didn't Do It Alone*, pp. 19-20.

[230]Source: Sean McCann, compiler, *The Wit of Oscar Wilde*, p. 10, 125.

[231]Source: Angelica Shirley Carpenter and Jean Shirley, *Frances Hodgson Burnett: Beyond the Secret Garden*, p. 88.

[232]Source: Janice Tingum, *E.B. White: The Elements of a Writer*, p. 39.

[233]Source: Sylvia Whitman, *Get Up and Go! The History of American Road Travel*, p. 19.

[234]Source: Jack Mingo, *The Juicy Parts*, p. 126.

[235] Source: Banksy, *Wall and Piece*, pp. 8, 169, 202. Is the quote from Colonel Mervin Willet Gonin genuine? I don't know. His private papers are at the Imperial War Museum, but a search of the Web site on 3 April 2011 did not turn up this quote. Even if the quote is not genuine, I think it expresses a truth.

[236]Source: Adam Woog, *Magicians and Illusionists*, pp. 74-75, 79.

[237]Source: Adam Sykes and Iain Sproat, compilers, *The Wit of Westminster*, p. 68.

[238]Source: Glenhall Taylor, *Before Television*, p. 70.

[239]Source: Tom Mullen, *Laughing Out Loud and Other Religious Experiences*, p. 127.

[240]Source: Sylvia Whitman, *V is for Victory*, p. 31.

[241] Source: Luke Chan, *101 Lessons of Tao*, p. 55.

[242] Source: *Anecdotes of the Hour By Famous Men*, pp. 23, 70.

[243]Source: Adam Sykes and Iain Sproat, compilers, *The Wit of Westminster*, p. 109.

[244]Source: Kenneth Williams, *Acid Drops*, p. 97.

[245] Source: Martin Buber, *The Way of Man*, pp. 15-17.

[246]Source: Art Linkletter, *I Didn't Do It Alone*, p. 10.

[247] Source: John J. McPhaul, *Deadlines and Monkeyshines: The Fabled World of Chicago Journalism*, p. 37.

[248]Source: Fesquet, Henri, collector, *Wit and Wisdom of Good Pope John*, pp. 57, 71.

[249]Source: Glenhall Taylor, *Before Television*, pp. 35-36.

[250]Source: Wanda Rutkowska, *Famous People in Anecdotes*, p. 51.

[251]Source: Nahum N. Glatzer, editor, *Hammer on the Rock*, p. 13.